MEXICO

Torture with impunity

AI Index: AMR 41/04/91
ISBN: 0-939994-68-2
First published September 1991
Amnesty International USA
322 Eighth Avenue
New York, NY 10001

Printed by John D. Lucas Printing, USA

Copyright
  Amnesty International
  Publications
Original language English
All rights reserved
No part of this publication
may be reproduced, stored
in a retrieval system, or
transmitted in any form or by
any means electronic,
mechanical, photo-
copying, recording and/or
otherwise, without the prior
permission of the publishers

CONTENTS

	Page

	Introduction	1
1	**Torture: Victims, Perpetrators, Circumstances, And Methods**	5
	The victims of torture	6
	Perpetrators of torture	16
	Circumstances of torture	18
	Methods of torture	25
2	**Torture: The legal context**	27
	Legal prohibition of torture	27
	Official response to torture	29
	The National Human Rights Commission	30
3	**Factors Facilitating Torture**	37
	Mexican jurisprudence, criminal law and legal procedure	37
	Immunity from prosecution	42
	Ineffectiveness of legal remedies	45
4	**Amnesty International's Proposals To Prevent Torture**	48

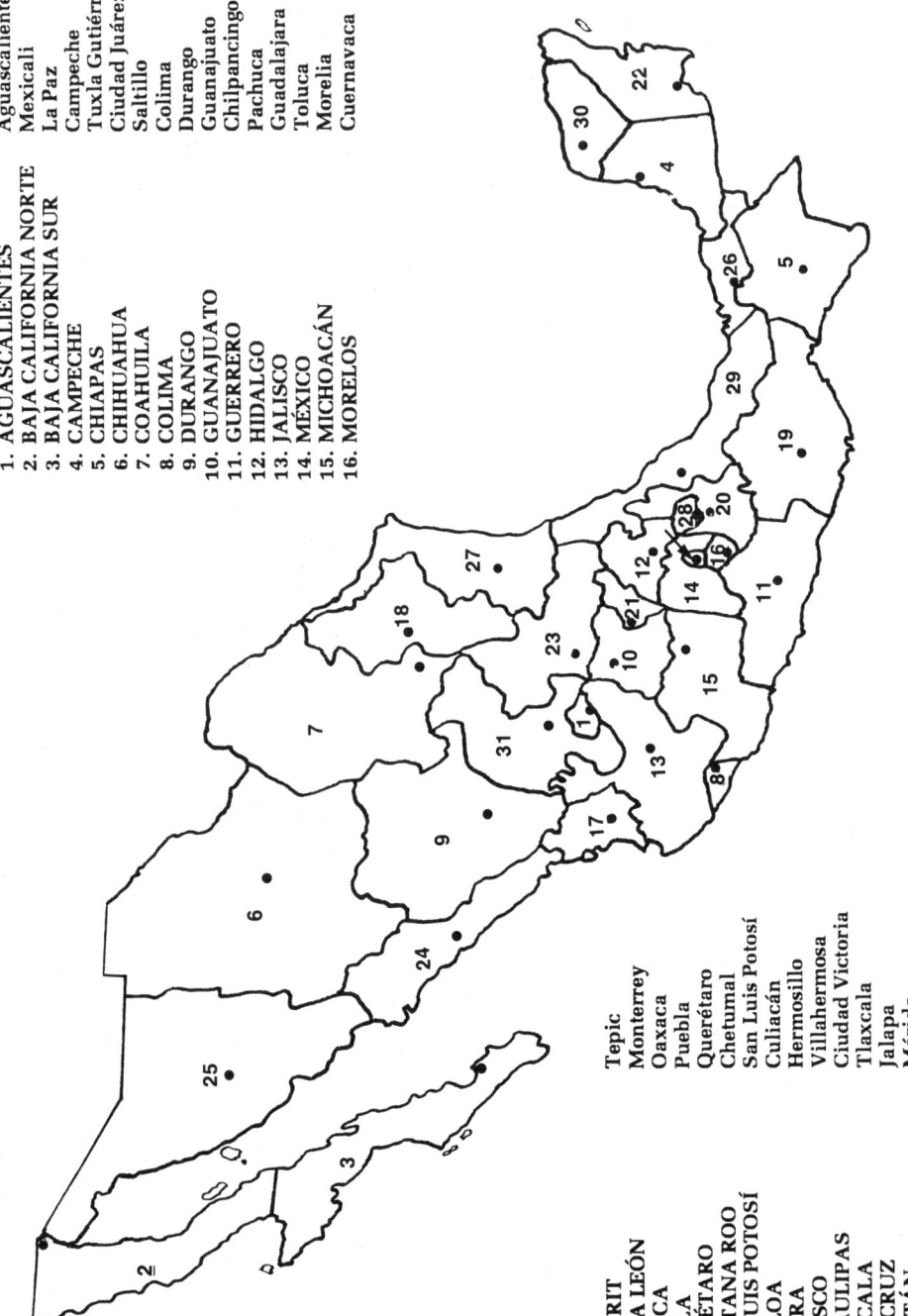

INTRODUCTION

In mid-1990 the Mexican Government faced a new wave of national and international criticism over the issue of human rights violations. It was triggered by the "death squad"-style killing of human rights lawyer Norma Corona Sapién on 21 May. She was president of the independent Commission for the Defence of Human Rights in Sinaloa state until shot dead in the state capital, Culiacán, by unidentified gunmen. At the time of her death she was investigating the case of a Mexican lawyer and three Venezuelan university professors, reportedly abducted by federal judicial police agents, who had been found dead near Culiacán in February 1990. Their bodies bore signs of torture.

In March 1990 Norma Corona Sapién had publicly announced that she was receiving death threats because of her investigations; threats which she believed came from federal police agents. The outrage which followed her murder led the Mexican Government to give a public commitment that "things would change" — that it would address the issue of widespread human rights violations, in particular torture.

One year later[1], despite the government's public prohibition of torture, and a series of legal and administrative initiatives, almost anyone arrested is at risk. Torture remains endemic in Mexico. Amnesty International believes the principal reason for this is the almost total impunity extended to law enforcement officers who routinely act beyond the law without fear of punishment.

The murder of Norma Corona Sapién was not the first time a Mexican Government had faced an outcry over its human rights record. Torture in Mexico became the focus of widespread publicity in September 1985. Evidence of torture was discovered as a result of an earthquake on 19 September which caused extensive loss of life and damage in the capital, Mexico City. One of the buildings destroyed was the headquarters of the Attorney General of the Federal District's Office. The Federal District includes the area in and around Mexico City. A number of dead bodies showing signs of torture were found in its ruins.

The public outcry which followed prompted the

---

1 This report was written in May 1991

MEXICO

Government of then President Miguel de la Madrid Hurtado to adopt a series of measures. These included the ratification, on 23 January 1986, of the United Nations (UN) Convention against Torture and Other Cruel, Inhuman or Degrading Treatment or Punishment. The Mexican Congress subsequently approved the Federal Law to Prevent and Punish Torture which explicitly defined torture by law enforcement agents as a crime and provided for the imprisonment of those found guilty. Despite these measures, Amnesty International continued to receive an increasing number of reports indicating that torture was widespread. In 1986 the organization had published a report on human rights violations in the rural areas of Oaxaca and Chiapas[2], where peasants and indigenous peoples were the victims of political killings, "disappearances", torture, and imprisonment on false criminal charges.

After President Carlos Salinas de Gortari took office in December 1988, the government embarked on a policy of enforcing "law and order". Measures were taken to tackle corruption in several spheres, including fraud and official involvement in drug trafficking — some 30 per cent of the Sinaloa state police force were dismissed because of their connections with the narcotics trade. Some human rights violations were also addressed. In June 1989 Antonio Zorilla Pérez, head of the security police under the de la Madrid government, was arrested in connection with the 1984 murder of investigative journalist Manuel Buendia; when he was killed the journalist had begun to uncover Zorilla's involvement in the drugs trade. During 1989 and early 1990 the government issued a series of official statements prohibiting torture.

An Amnesty International delegation visited Mexico between May and June 1990 to assess continuing reports of human rights violations by members of the Mexican law enforcement agencies and armed forces. The delegation interviewed dozens of people who had suffered or witnessed human rights violations: harassment, illegal detention, ill-treatment, arbitrary killings, extrajudicial executions, "disappearances" and, principally, torture. Much of the information contained in this report, which focuses specifically on torture and ill-treatment, is based on the findings of Amnesty International's delegation, updated by reports the organization continues to receive from Mexico. In addition to Amnesty International's own research, investigative work by independent human rights monitors in Mexico and by other international human rights organizations has also provided evidence that torture is widespread. In July 1990 the Campeche state Bar Association told the press that 99 per cent of criminal suspects detained in the state were tortured or ill-treated. The Bar Association's president, Wilberth Ortiz Cabañas, said that torture was used regularly to obtain confessions, and that the authorities were usually unresponsive to allegations that criminal defendants had confessed under duress. In August 1990 the

---

[2] *Mexico: Human rights violations in rural areas*, ISBN 086210 098 4; AI Index: AMR 41/07/86

INTRODUCTION

independent Bi-National Human Rights Centre, based in Tijuana, published a survey of dozens of prisoners in *La Mesa*, the Baja California Norte state penitentiary. The survey concluded that 99 per cent had been tortured or ill-treated by police officers after their arrest. Half said they were innocent of the charges against them but had confessed because they were tortured.

Growing public awareness of human rights issues in Mexico has stimulated the creation of independent organizations dedicated to the protection and promotion of human rights. In many Mexican states, particularly in the remote rural areas, these organizations are the most important source of information about human rights violations. In addition, independent human rights organizations have played an important role in helping victims in their search for redress. This work is not without risk. There can be little doubt that Norma Corona Sapién was murdered because of her investigations into gross human rights violations. Human rights monitors in other Mexican states have also received death threats because of their work.

The victims of torture are not limited to specific sectors of the population. They include people detained for political reasons or in the context of land disputes; human rights activists and those trying to investigate human rights abuses; people suspected of growing or trafficking in drugs; and people detained on suspicion of having carried out other criminal offences. Women and children have been tortured. Police officers have detained and tortured members of other police units and prison guards. Even a prison director is reported to have been tortured.

The same methods of torture are used throughout Mexico and in many cases reported to Amnesty International they have proved fatal. They are brutal methods — one teenager was beaten so savagely that, according to his mother, he scarcely reacted when two of his toenails were pulled out.

The pattern established by hundreds of cases is that when police officers are under pressure to solve a particular crime, they detain individuals targeted on suspicion of involvement in political or criminal activities, or else seize people at random on the streets, force them to confess to criminal offences under torture in incommunicado detention, and then obtain convictions by producing these confessions in court. Mexican courts have routinely admitted in evidence confessions made under torture by defendants accused of criminal offences, in spite of the fact that this is categorically prohibited by national and international law.

Torture is widespread, yet it is absolutely prohibited whatever the circumstances by Mexican law and by international human rights standards the government has sworn to uphold. There is ample legal provision at federal and state level to prevent and punish torture and it has been condemned at the highest level of government. At the inaugural ceremony of the governmental National Human Rights Commission, on 6 June 1990, President Salinas promised that the government would "confront the new threats to human rights wherever they come from...the political line of the Government of the Republic is to defend human rights and punish those who violate them; it is to end once and for all

MEXICO

any kind of impunity". The new commission was established to investigate and recommend action in cases of human rights violations, but was given neither the broad investigative powers nor the constitutional authority to effectively carry out these tasks.

Amnesty International believes the principal reason why torture continues to be widespread is the effective immunity from prosecution extended to law enforcement agents who commit the crime of torture. Hundreds of cases of torture by law enforcement agents, principally members of the federal and state police forces, have been reported to official bodies, independent human rights groups and to Amnesty International in recent years. Many of the cases are well-documented with testimonial, medical and forensic evidence, but those responsible have seldom been investigated and even more rarely prosecuted for the crime of torture.

The continuing and widespread use of torture, despite its prohibition at the highest levels of government, must call into question the political will behind the government's public commitment to end torture. Although Amnesty International welcomes the steps that the Mexican Government has taken to address this issue, these measures have failed to stop the practice of torture and ill-treatment in Mexico. Those responsible continue to benefit from impunity.

1

Torture: victims, perpetrators, circumstances, and methods

The victims of torture in Mexico come from most walks of life, but are usually from the poorest sections of the population. Most are men, but women and children have also been brutally tortured. Most are tortured in connection with criminal investigations or with police anti-drugs operations. Many of the victims of torture are political activists — recent years have seen increased attacks on political opponents of the government — and trade unionists. Some victims are human rights activists in the broadest sense of the term: victims' relatives seeking redress. Torture is widespread in the rural areas, although their remoteness means that it is less well-documented than torture in urban areas. Peasant and indigenous activists, often engaged in struggles for land rights, are frequently the victims. Even police officers have been tortured. On 17 January 1990 the Federal District Attorney General ordered an investigation into an incident in which 12 federal judicial police agents allegedly kidnapped and tortured two uniformed state judicial police officers. The 12 agents were suspended from duty pending investigation by the Public Ministry. Although the Attorney General of the Federal District said that they would be dismissed from the police force and brought to trial, over one year later no further developments had been reported.

People are most frequently tortured to force them to confess to criminal charges. People have also been tortured to deter them from pursuing complaints against the police, to make them give information about suspects and, in some cases, to extort money from them. On 20 March 1990 Oscar Humberto Castro Rodríguez, a farmer from Bellavista de Culiancito, Sinaloa, was detained by three federal judicial police officers in the town of Culiacán, taken to the local Republic Attorney General's Office, and tortured until he agreed to pay them 20 million pesos (approximately US $7,000). He was released the following day but said that the police officers had threatened to kill him if he complained about his treatment. Despite this he made an official complaint to the state Attorney General's Office and sought protection from the state authorities. He also took his case to the National Human Rights Commission, which recommended, on 18 June 1990, that two police officers be dismissed and possibly remanded. However, no action is known to have been taken against them.

MEXICO

Torture reportedly often begins at the moment of arrest and is a routine accompaniment to interrogation, during which detainees are usually held incommunicado. Torture usually continues until a confession has been extracted from the detainee.

The victims of torture

"They attached the wires, one to each foot — to each big toe — and when they connected them, I convulsed from the shocks. But before they did this they put a cloth in my mouth, and a *judicial*[1] grabbed me from behind and told me not to stick out my tongue because the electricity might make me bite it."

This is the testimony of a 17-year-old boy who claims he was tortured by state judicial police in Tijuana, Baja California Norte state. The torture of children during interrogation for criminal offences has been frequently reported in Tijuana. The victims are usually from the most disadvantaged sectors of society: homeless teenagers, the children of poor urban families and young rural migrants from the Mexican interior. They have neither the money nor the status to protect themselves from abuse. The methods of torture described include beatings and whippings with belts, electric torture, near-asphyxiation in water and with plastic bags over the head, mineral water forced into the nostrils and sexual abuse. Children have also been illegally imprisoned and tortured in *La Mesa*, the state penitentiary for adults in Tijuana. In April 1990 three juveniles imprisoned in *La Mesa*'s punishment cells claimed they were tortured. One of them, a 16-year-old girl, was two months pregnant and had a fractured nose as a result of beatings carried out, she alleged, by federal police officers. After the publicity given to her case, she was transferred to a women's prison. An official investigation into the allegations of torture and ill-treatment of children in Tijuana was opened in May 1990 but, at the time

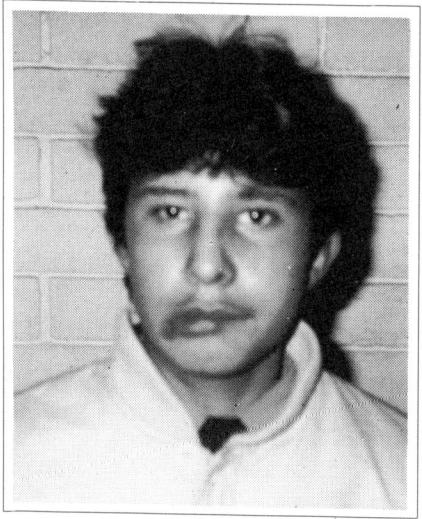

Fernando Nava González, 16, said he was repeatedly beaten on the face after his arrest by the state judicial police on 17 January 1990 in the town of Tijuana. He was remanded in custody under charges of theft.

---

1   Judicial police officer

CHAPTER 1

of writing, May 1991, those allegedly responsible had neither been arrested nor suspended from duty.

The torture and ill-treatment of children has frequently been reported in Baja California Norte state. In 1988 the independent Bi-National Human Rights Centre in Tijuana had published a report on the torture and ill-treatment of 108 minors between the ages of nine and 17 by state and federal judicial police and municipal police in Baja California Norte over a five-month period. Despite the filing of formal complaints in some of these cases and widespread publicity, no action is known to have been taken against those implicated in the abuses.

Reports of the torture of children have been received from several other states. On 22 January 1990 five children and one adult were detained by members of the state police in Simojovel, Chiapas state, while they were selling coffee. They were taken to the municipal auditorium, where they were allegedly tortured: their heads were pushed into the toilet bowl and they were threatened with pistols in an effort to make them confess to cultivating drugs. They were released without charge later the same day. The case received extensive publicity in the local news media but to Amnesty International's knowledge no details of any investigation have been made known.

In November 1989 inhabitants of Topilejo, Mexico state, made an official complaint that federal highway police officers had killed one peasant farmer and arrested and tortured three others, after apprehending them on suspicion of robbery. Two of the victims were children, Miguel Angel García Chávez and Arturo Monroy, who alleged that after their arrest, on 20 November, they were tortured by beatings, kicks and blows and by having mineral water forced up their nostrils, and were threatened with "disappearance", in order to force them to sign blank statements. The police officers involved were arrested and charged with abuse of authority but subsequently released on bail. As of May 1991 no further action was known to have been taken.

Joaquín Capetillo Santana was detained by state judicial police agents on suspicion of robbery on 10 May 1986 in Villahermosa, Tabasco state. He was then 13 years old. During the following days he was reportedly tortured in custody at the local police headquarters and forced to confess to several crimes. The torture allegedly consisted of beatings, near-asphyxiation in water and electric shocks to several parts of the body, including the testicles. Nine days later, the police presented him to the media as a dangerous criminal and he was transferred to the local prison for adults, the Centre for Social Rehabilitation, instead of the juvenile centre.

At the time of writing, Joaquín Capetillo Santana was still in detention in the Centre for Social Rehabilitation in Villahermosa, awaiting trial. During his imprisonment he has reportedly suffered beatings and threats, both from prison wardens and adult prisoners.

The Mexican Constitution stipulates that detainees should be tried within four months of arrest, when the maximum penalty for the offence does not exceed two years' imprisonment; and within one year, if the maximum penalty is greater. The imprisonment of minors in adult prisons is forbidden by the Constitution.

MEXICO

The arbitrary arrest and torture of the government's critics and political opponents has frequently been reported.

Martín Sebastián Peña Mejía, a member of the Revolutionary Democratic Party (PRD), a legal opposition party founded in 1989, was arrested without a warrant on 9 February 1990 in Jonacatepec, Morelos state, and held incommunicado for five days by the state police. He later stated that he was beaten and tortured by near-asphyxiation and having water forced up his nose, and threatened by the police who demanded he confess to various crimes. A forensic report on Martín Sebastián Peña Mejía's physical condition conducted 10 days after his arrest is consistent with his allegations of torture. In one of several threats, one of his torturers reportedly told him that he would suffer the "same fate as other rotten politicians", naming Timoteo Mardonio Estudillo Piña, Esteban Morales and Marcos Rivera, who were killed during 1989 and 1990, and José Ramón García Gómez, who "disappeared" in 1989. In all four cases official involvement was alleged. It appears that Martín Sebastián Peña Mejía was arrested and tortured because of his political activities. He was released without charge after local supporters marched to the police headquarters in Jonacatepec where he was held and requested that his detention be acknowledged. On 14 February Martín Sebastián Peña Mejía presented a formal complaint about his arrest and alleged torture to the local authorities. As of May 1991 no investigations in his case have been reported to Amnesty International.

In March 1990 a PRD leader in Guerrero state was released on the orders of the state governor after he claimed he had been forced to confess to false charges under torture. Eloy Cisneros Guillén alleged that he and his brother, Ladislao Cisneros Guillén, were arrested by state police without warrants on 6 March 1990 in Acapulco, the state capital, and beaten and tortured by near-asphyxiation. He said he had been forced to make a statement without the presence of a lawyer. He was then taken with his brother to the Centre for Social Rehabilitation in Acapulco. The prison director admitted that Eloy Cisneros Guillén had to be hospitalized on the day he was brought to the prison and that the medical report showed he had some bruising. Although both men were released without charge on the state governor's orders, no inquiry into their allegations of torture had been reported at the time of writing.

Students have also been tortured. Gastón González Gutiérrez, a student leader in the law faculty of the Autonomous University of Tamaulipas state, was reportedly detained by the state judicial police in Tampico in March 1990. He claims he was beaten and threatened in custody to force him to confess to a murder. Three other students, Eduardo Martínez Szymanski, Miguel González Gutiérrez and Ignacio Ramírez, are said to have confessed to the crime under torture. As of May 1991 no investigation into their allegations of torture had been reported.

Trade union activists have been detained and interrogated under torture about their activities. In December 1989 two teachers, both active members of the National Education Workers' Union (SNTE) section in Tuxtla Gutiérrez, Chiapas state, were reportedly arrested and tortured by members of the federal judicial

CHAPTER 1

police. Rubicel Einstein Ruiz Gamboa, aged 29, and Oscar de Jesús Peña Esquinca, aged 36, both leaders of a dissident wing of the union, had participated in a demonstration in November at the offices of the state Public Education Ministry, in Tuxtla Gutiérrez. They and other union activists were held responsible for disturbances which occurred during the demonstration.

The teachers claimed they were arrested without warrants by five or six police agents in Tuxtla Gutiérrez on 15 December, forced into an unmarked vehicle and driven off. Both teachers said they were hooded, beaten and threatened throughout their ordeal. Their abductors identified themselves as members of the federal police and questioned the teachers about a list of other union activists.

The teachers said they were driven to an area in the countryside, which they recognized as the Grijalba River gorge, and there threatened with being thrown over the precipice because of their trade union activities. Later that day they were taken to the Attorney General's Office in Tuxtla Gutiérrez where arrest warrants were issued on charges of damage to federal property, aggression and theft: charges they denied. They were then taken to *Cerro Hueco*, the state prison, in Tuxtla Gutiérrez, where they remained for the next five months. Once in prison they suffered no further ill-treatment. However, their requests for medical examinations to certify the treatment they had suffered were reportedly denied.

Both teachers were released on 26 May 1990 after the charges against

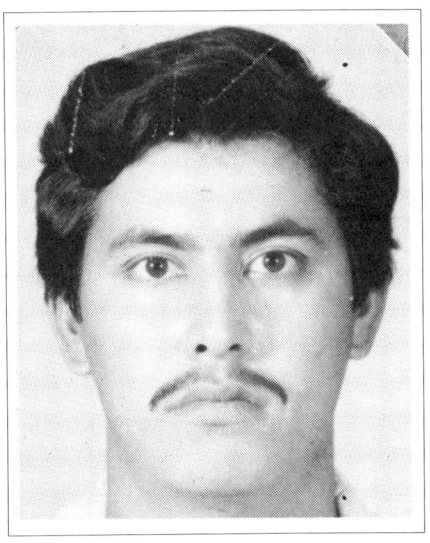

(Above) Rubicel Einstein Ruiz Gamboa, one of two teachers arrested and reportedly tortured after taking part in a trade union protest. They were detained for five months and then released. (Below) Street poster demanding the teachers' release. The case against them was dropped after a campaign by local branches of the teachers' trade union.

9

MEXICO

them were dropped when the state Public Education Ministry abandoned its complaint against the two. However, at the time of writing, May 1991, no investigation into their allegations of torture had been reported.

In another case, nine teachers in the state of Michoacán are awaiting trial on charges of damage to federal property, theft and aggression; charges which are apparently based solely on confessions given under torture. They were among a group of 102 members of the local section of the SNTE who were arrested in Morelia on 3 July 1990 during a demonstration demanding higher wages and protesting against their union's official policy on education, which they claimed to be biased in favour of the government. During the demonstration the teachers surrounded the offices of the state Public Education Ministry occupied the SNTE premises in Morelia, and reportedly harassed two visiting representatives of SNTE national headquarters.

According to reports, all 102 teachers were taken into custody by federal and state judicial police. They were held incommunicado for two days at the state police headquarters. During that time they were reportedly questioned about their political activities and many were said to have been tortured and threatened with death.

Most of the teachers were released without charge. Seventeen were transferred on 6 July to the Morelia state prison with charges apparently based solely on their confessions. On 6 August 1990 the charges against eight of them were dropped and they were released. Amnesty International has seen medical reports on some of the teachers who were released without charge. The findings of these reports are consistent with the torture described — chiefly beatings and near-asphyxiation with plastic bags.

The nine teachers still detained and awaiting further trial proceedings are active members of the local section of the SNTE. At the time of writing, May 1991, no investigations have been reported into the teachers' allegations of torture, and no police officers have been charged.

Braulio Aguilar Reyes, aged 23, an independent union activist, was detained on 29 April 1991 on the outskirts of Mexico City by two unidentified armed men who intercepted the car he was driving. According to his sister, María Alejandra Aguilar, who was with him in the car, the two men forced Braulio Aguilar Reyes out without an explanation and drove him away in another vehicle. His reported abduction resulted in a public outcry demanding his release.

Braulio Aguilar Reyes' whereabouts remained unknown until the following day when his relatives received a call from someone who claimed to have seen him in detention in the *Delegación Miguel Hidalgo*, a federal district judicial police station in Mexico City. His detention was acknowledged after his relatives made an official complaint and he was released at midnight. According to reports, he had been held incommunicado and given no reasons for his detention. He was reportedly tortured with beatings, blows and kicks, causing multiple bruises, spinal injuries and a ruptured ear-drum, which required urgent medical treatment after his release. He was also allegedly threatened because of his political activities.

CHAPTER 1

After Braulio Aguilar Reyes was released two federal district judicial police agents allegedly involved in his torture were arrested. Their legal situation was still unclear at the time of writing. Braulio Aguilar Reyes' relatives have requested that the activities of other people allegedly involved in his abduction and torture be investigated. According to reports, Braulio Aguilar Reyes and his brother, Gustavo, also an independent union activist, had received several threats from members of the official Mexican Republic's Petroleum Workers' Union, because of their leadership role in an independent rank and file trade union movement demanding adequate compensation for the former employees of a refinery on the outskirts of Mexico City, who lost their jobs when the refinery was closed, in March 1991, as part of a much publicized governmental action to curb pollution in Mexico City, in accordance with environmental measures required by the proposed NAFTA (North American Free Trade Agreement).

Human rights activists have also been tortured. Salomón Mendoza Barajas, the mayor of Aguililla in Michoacán state, and a PRD member, was detained and reportedly tortured when he complained about human rights violations committed during anti-drugs operations in his region. The events which led to his arrest began on 5 May 1990 when agents of the federal police drug-squad raided the peasant community of Ayacata, in the municipality of Aguililla. According to reports there was an armed confrontation between the police and the peasants, during which a five-year-old child and a police agent were killed. The following day, federal police officers raided the town of Aguililla to capture those responsible for the agent's death, and seized 55 people, one of whom, it was later disclosed, died in their custody.

After the raid Salomón Mendoza Barajas went to the military barracks where the federal police station was sited to complain to the commander about the abuses inflicted on the inhabitants of Aguililla. He was arrested on the spot, without a warrant, and tortured in the military barracks under police custody, according to his testimony. He described being first beaten on the face and testicles, then, blindfold and bound, taken to a room where he was pushed to the floor and repeatedly kicked and stepped on; a plastic bag was placed over his head while he was punched in the face and stomach.

Later that day, Salomón Mendoza Barajas was transferred to Mexico City, while the federal police searched his house in Aguililla and, according to his wife, María del Carmen Contreras Cervantes, "planted" a small plastic bag containing seeds and some white powder, which they took away as evidence. She said the agents returned the following day with more drugs and arms which were placed in a cupboard in the house and then photographed.

In Mexico City Salomón Mendoza Barajas was held in a cell at the Republic Attorney General's Office for two days where he said he was ill-treated by the police and forced to sign documents without knowing their contents. He was then transferred to the East Preventive Detention Centre in Mexico City where he learned he had signed a confession to charges of murder, illegal possession of arms and drugs and criminal association with drug-traffickers. A detention order was issued on 13 May, on the basis of these charges.

MEXICO

Salomón Mendoza Barajas was interviewed and medically examined by Amnesty International delegates during a visit to Mexico in May 1990. According to the forensic doctor who examined him, Salomón Mendoza Barajas was suffering from: acute chronic pain and motor impairment of the right shoulder resulting from trauma caused by a blunt instrument; slight paralysis of both lower limbs consistent with injuries to the lower vertebral column; recent scars on the nasal bridge; recent scars on the left wrist consistent with abrasive injuries. The medical findings were consistent with his allegations of torture.

Salomón Mendoza Barajas, a local mayor, was reportedly brutally tortured and charged with drug offences and murder after he complained about arbitrary detentions and police harassment. A public campaign secured his release

This case was one of several about which Amnesty International expressed its concerns during a meeting with a representative of the governmental National Human Rights Commission who visited the organization's London headquarters in November 1990. On 28 November 1990 the National Human Rights Commission issued a report on the abuses suffered by the inhabitants of Aguililla in May, and presented a series of recommendations to the Attorney General's Office. The commission recommended dropping the charges and unconditionally releasing Salomón Mendoza Barajas and three others arrested during the raid: Javier Rosiles Martínez, Magdaleno Vera García and Carlos Valencia Morfín. It also recommended dropping charges of drug-trafficking against Francisco Valencia Vargas, Luis Elisea Valencia, Jerónimo Madrigal Guízar, Francisco Pérez Alcázar, Miguel Pérez Alcázar and Luis Revueltas González, all of whom had been released pending trial. The commission requested that the alleged abuses by the federal judicial police in Aguililla be investigated and that those responsible be brought to justice.

On 10 December 1990 the charges against Salomón Mendoza Barajas and Javier Rosiles Martínez were dropped by the Republic Attorney General's Office and they were both released. The charges against the other prisoners were not dropped; two of them, Carlos Valencia Morfín and Magdaleno Vera García, are still in prison awaiting trial. At the time of writing, May 1991, no judicial investigation of the abuses had been reported, nor had the federal police agents implicated been charged.

Torture in rural Mexico has been widely reported for many years and was the subject of an Amnesty International report in 1986. Now, as then, many of the victims are peasants and indigenous peoples active in the struggle for land rights.

Zócimo Centeno Hernández, a 23-year-old peasant active in campaigns for land

CHAPTER 1

rights in Ilamatlán in the state of Veracruz, is currently awaiting trial on charges of murder and criminal association based on a confession he claims to have made under torture. He was detained by state police in November 1989 and first taken to a private house in Ilamatlán where, he claims, he was interrogated about various crimes, including the murder of Pedro Hernández, a local peasant activist. The torture he described consisted of blows to his abdomen and genitals and near-asphyxiation in water, and having his head covered with a plastic bag. He was then taken to the local jail in Ilamatlán where, he said, he continued to be tortured with blows, near-asphyxiation and electric shocks until he agreed to sign a statement saying he was involved in a series of murders. From Ilamatlán he was taken to Huayacocotla where he was interrogated in the local police station about his participation in peasant organizations and threatened with "disappearance". He was finally taken to the state police headquarters in Jalapa, where he alleged he was tortured again and questioned about his involvement in political activities.

He is now awaiting trial in Huayacocotla prison. He believes his role in land struggles is the reason why he has been detained, tortured and charged and says he has an alibi to prove he is innocent of the murder of Pedro Hernández. He is being legally represented by a public defence counsel. His statement apparently will be used as evidence against him.

Peasant women have also been tortured and ill-treated. Two pregnant women were among 15 members of the Irapuato Popular Settlements Union (UCOPI), an organization prominent in the defence of peasants' land rights in Irapuato, Guanajuato state, who were detained without warrants by the public security police for several hours in January 1990. The detainees said they were tortured, threatened with death and forced to put their fingerprints to statements they were unable to read because they are illiterate. They were released without charge. Both women said that they were beaten on the stomach in custody and one of them, Amalia Chávez Negrete, reportedly miscarried as a result. Another woman was reportedly shut in a room, partially undressed, and then pushed out into the street in her underwear. The men were warned to look after the women, otherwise the women would be raped. In March 1990 UCOPI leader Eduardo Martín Negrete publicly accused a named official of ordering the abuses that occurred in Irapuato in January and said that UCOPI leaders had subsequently been harassed and received death threats. No investigations into the allegations have been reported.

There have been frequent reports of the torture of indigenous people, and particularly of leading members of indigenous organizations. Juan Martínez Pérez, a leader of the Movement for Triqui Unity and Struggle (MULT) in the Triqui Indian region of San Juan Copala, state of Oaxaca, was arrested by members of the preventive police, a branch of the state police, on 11 September 1988 and accused of murder. The police reportedly did not produce an arrest warrant and beat him over the head with their weapons. Another MULT leader, Margarito Méndez Hernández, was arrested with him and the two were transferred to the custody of a group of civilian gunmen and soldiers from the 48th battalion based in San Juan Copala and taken to Juxtlahuaca. The two men were then handed over to the state judicial police to be transferred to the state capital, Oaxaca. On the way the police stopped in a layby where they reportedly tortured the two men with beatings and threatened to throw them over a cliff because of their activities in the MULT. In Oaxaca, the detainees were taken to the state Attorney General's Office and were once again beaten and threatened. They confessed to the murder charges reportedly as a result of their treatment and were placed at the disposition of the courts who ordered their detention in the state penitentiary in Oaxaca. At the time of writing they were still awaiting trial.

Another MULT leader from San Juan Copala, Mateo Francisco Bautista, was also arrested on 11 September 1988 and accused of murder. He was transferred to Oaxaca at the same time as Juan Martínez and Margarito Méndez and is believed to have been treated in a similar fashion.

Juan Hernández de Jesús, 50-year-old peasant and MULT leader in Unión de los Angeles, was arrested at his home on 19 October 1989 by soldiers from the 48th battalion and accused of murder. He was reportedly beaten and threatened at his home and while being transferred to Juxtlahuaca. He speaks no Spanish and was not provided with an interpreter at the time of questioning. He is currently in the state penitentiary in Oaxaca pending trial.

Often the only means torture victims have to seek redress is the help of their relatives. Relatives who try to help have been threatened, harassed and sometimes tortured. According to reports, this is what happened to Guadalupe López Juárez whose 19-year-old son, Ricardo, died after being tortured by the police. Ricardo López, a labourer, was arrested in Mexico City on 22 March 1990 by members of the Gustavo A. Madero unit of the Federal District judicial police, and accused of kidnapping a young child and demanding a ransom. He remained in custody for three months and was repeatedly tortured until his death at the end of June.

When Ricardo López was first detained he was held incommunicado and his whereabouts were unknown. During this period he is believed to have confessed to the kidnapping as a result of torture. Five days after his arrest his mother, aunt and uncle were detained for 48 hours by members of the same police unit and interrogated about the kidnapped child's whereabouts with beatings and threats. At the same time the police presented Ricardo López to the media as the kidnapper and claimed he had told them where he had hidden the child's body. They had not located it, however.

Ricardo López was formally charged with the kidnapping on the basis of his confession and sent to the North Preventive Detention Centre in Mexico City. Here he continued to be tortured for information on the child's whereabouts. When his mother visited him at the beginning of May she saw that he had been severely beaten and that his left hand seemed to be fractured. Guadalupe López told the prison wardens that she was going to present a formal complaint about her son's condition. In the early hours of the following morning she was visited by members of the Federal District police and threatened with death if she

CHAPTER 1

pursued the complaint or visited her son. She was so frightened by this that she moved house.

In mid-May Guadalupe López received a letter from her son. He told her again that he was innocent and that his confession had been extracted under torture. He said he had been told by his torturers that he was going to be killed, and that he was frightened for his family. He begged her to visit him. When she went to visit him in prison at the beginning of June she found he was not there. Federal District police agents had taken him from the prison to an unknown destination for further questioning. They had done so illegally, without the consent of a judge, but Guadalupe López did not make a formal complaint because of the threats she had received the previous month.

On 22 June Guadalupe López was abducted on the street by armed members of the Federal District police and forced into a vehicle. The following sequence of events is described in her testimony. Ricardo, her son, was in the same vehicle and in bad physical condition. The two were taken handcuffed and blindfold to a house where they were stripped naked and their blindfolds were taken off. Their captors told them they were police agents investigating the kidnapping. Mother and son were then handcuffed to a pipe in the bathroom. Guadalupe López says that at this point her son was semi-conscious, with cigarette burns on several parts of his body, open wounds and a badly fractured foot. For the next two days mother and son were repeatedly tortured for information about the kidnapping. They were pushed into water tanks connected to the electricity mains and given electric shocks. Their heads were repeatedly forced into a toilet bowl containing excrement. They were beaten, threatened, burned with cigarettes, denied food and water, and subjected to mock executions. One of their torturers was a woman they recognized as a *madrina*[2].

On the third day of this ordeal — 24 June — Ricardo López was tortured so severely that he lost consciousness several times and, according to his mother, hardly reacted to the torture even when two of his toenails were pulled out. One of the senior officials present ordered the session to stop. He also warned Guadalupe López not to make a complaint.

That night, Guadalupe López and her son were driven to a place close to their former home and she was thrown out of the vehicle. Witnesses to the incident called an ambulance which took her to a local hospital. She was unconscious for three days and did not see her son alive again.

Ricardo López apparently died on the way back to the prison. His body was handed over to prison officials at 11pm that night, 24 June. It appears that police agents and prison officials then dressed the body and tried to make it look as if Ricardo López had committed suicide.

As soon as they learned what had happened to Guadalupe López, the family

---

2   Police informer

MEXICO

requested information about Ricardo López' whereabouts from the authorities. This was denied them, but on 29 June, after an extensive search, the family discovered his body in the mortuary of the local medical examiners' office. It was registered as unidentified and it bore signs of trauma, burns and cuts. Two toenails were missing. The death certificate stated the cause of death was "asphyxiation due to strangling following multiple trauma". Guadalupe López was unable to attend the funeral because of the serious injuries she had suffered under torture.

The family complained to the authorities and on 29 June 1990 the deputy chief of the Homicide Investigations Attorney's Office of the Gustavo A. Madero Unit of the Federal District Attorney General's Office was arrested and charged with complicity in murder and abuse of power. Three other police agents were also arrested on charges of causing injuries, abuse of authority and homicide and at the time of writing, May 1991, were standing trial. According to statements made by the other police officers, the deputy chief had given the orders for "necessary pressure" to be exerted on Ricardo López in order to obtain information about the child's whereabouts. However, the deputy chief was later released on bail. This provoked a public outcry and demands that all those responsible should be brought to justice.

On 19 September 1990 new charges were brought against the deputy chief and he was taken back into custody. The charges were abuse of authority and aggravated bodily harm, but he was again released on bail in January 1991. He was rearrested on 13 April 1991 and charged with the murder of Ricardo López. He claimed that his arrest was "unconstitutional", on the grounds that he had been arrested twice for the same offence. His claim was rejected by the judge in charge of the case who also ordered the arrest of a *madrina* allegedly involved in torturing Ricardo López. Several other people believed to share responsibility for the torture and murder of Ricardo López, including the prison director and the prison's security chief, had not been charged in connection with the case at the time of writing, May 1991.

Ricardo López' relatives reportedly received several anonymous threats after they presented complaints about the case. As a result, they have made public appeals to President Salinas, the Republic Attorney General's Office and the Federal District Attorney General, asking them to take measures to end the harassment. It is not known if the authorities took any action but the threats reportedly stopped several weeks after the complaints were filed.

Perpetrators of torture

The forces most frequently cited in reports of torture are the federal judicial police and the state judicial police, who carry out criminal investigations under the command of the federal or state Public Ministry or prosecutor's office. The Public Ministry is a branch of the Attorney General's Office which is in turn responsible to the executive power. Less frequently cited in reports of torture

CHAPTER 1

are the state preventive police, the public security police, the municipal police, the federal highway police, and the Directorate of Protection and Highways.

However, it is the federal judicial police, particularly the branch in charge of anti-narcotics investigations, who have most consistently been held responsible for human rights abuses including illegal detention, ill-treatment, torture, arbitrary killings and extrajudicial executions as well as harassment and extortion directed at detainees. These abuses are widespread and well-documented yet their perpetrators appear to be largely immune from investigation or prosecution; they enjoy an impunity which, Amnesty International believes, creates a climate conducive to further human rights violations by law enforcement officials.

Soldiers of the Mexican army have also been implicated in human rights violations, such as illegal detention, torture and arbitrary killings of detainees, particularly during anti-narcotics investigations in rural areas.

Eleazar Beltrán García, who lives in the southern mountainous region of the state of Chihuahua, was arrested for unknown reasons in August 1989 by an army unit from the military base at El Tascate, on the border between the states of Chihuahua and Durango. He later made official complaints to the Military Attorney General, the Republic Attorney General and the General Human Rights Directorate, as well as to the civilian authorities in Chihuahua and Durango about his treatment.

According to his testimony, after his arrest Eleazar Beltrán García was blindfolded, and his feet and hands were tied. He was then taken by a pick-up truck to the barracks at El Tascate where, "with my eyes still blindfolded and my hands tied, they stripped me and threw cold water over me. Then they put a plastic bag over my head so that I couldn't breathe. They also tied a rope round my neck, which was gradually tightened until I felt that my head was going to burst open. They continued to pour water over me and beat me all over. While they were doing this, they threatened me, saying that when the captain came, he would kill me. Later on a man appeared...he was a civilian who lived near the military base. He told me to be careful or I would be in trouble. During the night they introduced a bottle between my testicles and underpants, I was beaten and cold water was thrown over me. The next day...the civilian returned. He kicked me, threw cold water over me, seized hold of my head and forced water into my nose. Then he placed a rope around my neck, strung me up and left".

Eleazar Beltrán García said he was then hung up by the arms and told by the soldiers that he was going to die. He remained hanging by his arms for several hours until a senior officer arrived and ordered the soldiers to release him. Before he was released, Eleazar Beltrán García was warned that if he complained to the authorities his wife and daughters would be raped and killed.

At the time of writing, May 1991, Amnesty International had received no information about action taken in response to Eleazar Beltrán García's complaints to the authorities.

In a more recent case, Alvaro Martínez Quiñones, a peasant, was found dead four days after being detained by the army in Tepehuanes, Durango state. He had been arrested on 5 March 1990 in connection with a drugs offence. The army

MEXICO

claimed that he had committed suicide after they had released him from custody. A formal complaint about the case was made in the state congress by local representatives and passed to the congressional Justice Committee. The circumstances of Alvaro Martínez Quiñones' death remained unclarified at the time of writing, in May 1991.

Human rights abuses are also committed by civilians unofficially recruited and working under the direction of the judicial police. They are known as *madrinas*, *soplones* or *informantes*, a variety of terms used to describe police informers. These civilians carry weapons and appear to collaborate principally with the federal police. They are alleged to have been responsible for abuses such as illegal arrests, ill-treatment, torture, arbitrary killings and extrajudicial executions. They are reported to enjoy the protection of the police forces that recruit them. They are rarely prosecuted and are largely immune from police disciplinary procedures. Mexico is obliged under the UN Convention against Torture to prosecute all public officials or people acting in an official capacity who inflict, instigate, consent to, or acquiesce in torture.

In July 1989 the state Attorney General of San Luis Potosí said that his office was still receiving complaints that judicial police agents, including *madrinas*, and the federal police commander were committing abuses. He referred to a complaint he said he had recently received from the inhabitants of the community of Antón de los Martínez in the municipality of Tierra Nueva, after armed federal judicial police agents and *madrinas* arrived in the community and said that they were searching for marijuana growers. They detained five people, including the local municipal police chief, and reportedly beat them and forced mineral water up their nostrils. Amnesty International has not received information about any prosecutions of those responsible.

Circumstances of torture

Torture has been primarily reported in the context of criminal investigations including anti-narcotics operations; its main purpose appears to be to intimidate detainees and obtain confessions. Confessions continue to have high evidential value in the courts and in many cases reported to Amnesty International they have been the only evidence on which defendants have been convicted, despite their allegations that their statements of guilt had been obtained under torture.

Torture is usually carried out in police stations and Public Ministry offices but reports indicate that it is sometimes practised at places other than official detention centres, such as hotels, car parks, or deserted rural areas.

Twenty-one-year-old Emiliano Olivas Madrigal was reportedly detained without an arrest warrant by the federal judicial police on 18 October 1989 in San Francisco de la Joya, municipality of Guadalupe y Calvo, Chihuahua state, and taken to a hotel room rented by the police. He was found dead the next day, in handcuffs, near the hotel. According to a doctor who saw the body, it had marks on the chest similar to cigarette burns, and bruising consistent with other forms

CHAPTER 1

of torture. The hotel owner said that guests had complained during the night that they could hear shouting and banging in one of the rooms. After the body was found, the same police agents are said to have detained another man, Enrique Luna, whom they paraded about the village with a hood over his head. According to Teresa Jardí, a lawyer representing the Chihuahua Commission on Solidarity and Defence of Human Rights, an autopsy performed on Emiliano Olivas Madrigal's body showed he had been brutally tortured and witnesses had said he was thrown from the third floor of the hotel. Three federal police officers were later suspended, arrested, and charged with homicide in connection with the killing of Emiliano Olivas Madrigal. At the time of writing, May 1991, Amnesty International had received no information as to whether they were tried and convicted.

"It was like a nightmare. They arrived at three in the morning at my friend's house and after searching the house, and assaulting my wife, my friend's wife and our children, they accused us of being drug-traffickers. In front of his children, they placed a plastic bag on my friend's head. The way he started to suffocate was like a horror film...He was purple and the plastic bag was almost stuck to his face. His children were crying. His wife tried to stop them torturing him but they pushed her away, hitting her. They put my hands behind my back and covered me with a blanket and started beating me. We couldn't believe it. 'Where are the drugs?' they asked us, accompanying their demands with endless insults and blows. They insulted our wives. And they also beat them, as if they were men."

This description of a drugs raid in November 1989 was given by lawyer Antonio Partida Valdovinos, a former president of the Tepic Bar Association, in Nayarit state, and former vice-president of the National Federation of Bar Associations. He says that he confessed to drugs offences in order to stop the federal judicial police suffocating his friend and beating both men's wives.

The house was raided and Antonio Partida and his friend were arrested after the lawyer had visited the Federal District police headquarters in Mexico City to inquire about a client. He subsequently gave the following account about his treatment to journalists, and to the third district judge, before whom he appeared after 10 days in incommunicado detention.

After Antonio Partida had confessed he and his friend, Antonio Murray, were taken to the cells at the Attorney General's Office, and, later that day, by plane to his house in the countryside where he had told the police the drugs were stored. "I went fearing that they were going to kill us. There were no drugs. They didn't exist. When we got to the house, accompanied by more than 40 agents, armed to the teeth, my panic was uncontrollable. We went in. The blows were brutal. 'Where are the drugs?' they asked. 'There'. I pointed to a room. They went in — and as I knew they would — found nothing. Then there began a real orgy of violence. They all beat us. They threw me to the ground and began to kick me and my friend. They took me by the feet and, with a plastic bag on my head, put me in the swimming pool. They kept on for hours...They said they were waiting for our accomplices, who never arrived because they simply did not exist. Before

MEXICO

boarding the plane to return to Mexico City, they said they would throw us out of it. 'No one knows about you or us. The same will happen to your families.'..."

Both men were charged with drugs offences, apparently on the basis of their confessions, and taken to the East Preventive Detention Centre, in Mexico City. There Antonio Partida was interviewed by a journalist from the newspaper *Excelsior* a few days later. According to the journalist, his arms, legs and back were bruised and he was suffering from severe pain in the ribs. Both Antonio Partida and Antonio Murray have presented official complaints about their treatment to the Attorney General's Office. They are still awaiting trial and, according to information available to Amnesty International, those responsible for the torture have not been brought to justice. This case prompted a public outcry and protest from several Bar Associations who protested that lawyers had been frequent targets of human rights violations by law enforcement agents and called on President Salinas, on 4 December 1989, for guarantees of respect of their rights.

During 1989 and 1990 reports of torture in the context of anti-narcotics investigations caused such public concern that President Salinas was forced to publicly address the issue. In July 1990 he condemned the practice of human rights violations in the context of anti-narcotics investigations as a source of corruption and attacks against freedom. At the same time, he announced some administrative measures intended to curb the problem. He said both federal and state judicial police agents would be required to carry proper identification, that the police would be prohibited from using unofficial cars and that random road blocks by the police would be discontinued.

Despite this announcement, torture of those suspected of drugs offences continued and in some cases led to the death of the victim.

Pedro Yescas Martínez, aged 34, died in detention in the state capital of Durango on 8 October 1990, five days after his arrest by the federal judicial police. According to several eye-witnesses, he was severely tortured and forced to confess to drug charges during his detention and was later denied adequate medical treatment for the serious injuries he had sustained under torture. A public outcry and complaints by his relatives prompted an official investigation but those responsible had not been brought to justice as of May 1991.

Javier Delgado Gutiérrez, aged 48, was detained by several federal police agents in Guadalajara, Jalisco state, on 2 October 1990 on suspicion of being a drugs dealer. Later that day he underwent a routine examination by two forensic doctors in the local federal police office. They reported that he was "tachycardiac[3] and restless", which they attributed to drug addiction, and described bruises on several parts of his body, which they said had occurred before his

---

3   Displaying abnormal rapidity of heart-beat

CHAPTER 1

detention and posed no risk to his life. Javier Delgado Gutiérrez died in custody later that night.

The police issued a public statement attributing his death to a heart attack, but a forensic examination of the body, carried out at the request of the National Human Rights Commission, found that he had died as a result of torture: his face was badly injured, his body, including the testicles, was heavily bruised, and his right ankle was fractured. Two federal police agents were arrested and charged with murder but several others allegedly involved have been neither charged nor disciplined — among them the senior officer of the group.

Two months later this senior officer was again implicated in human rights violations. A group of anti-narcotics federal police agents under his command killed six unarmed civilians, two of them children, when they reportedly opened fire without warning on a van in which, they later claimed, they believed drug-traffickers were travelling. The incident occurred on 2 December 1990 in the village of Angostura, Sinaloa state. The federal police agents and their senior officers were arrested and charged with murder. However, the Republic Attorney General's Office stated that this was a case of negligent homicide, not of murder, and announced that it would pay for the legal defence of those accused. The case is currently before the courts.

Nationals of other countries have also been arrested and tortured in connection with anti-narcotics investigations.

In May 1990 Amnesty International delegates visiting Mexico interviewed a Colombian student who described an incident earlier that month in which he, another Colombian student and a Mexican student were detained and tortured on the pretext of investigating their involvement in drug-trafficking. Their names cannot be made public for fear of reprisals.

The two Colombian students were apprehended outside a metro station in Mexico City, late one evening, by four men in civilian clothes who identified themselves as judicial police officers and forced them into a van at gunpoint. When the students produced their identity papers, the police agents realized that they were Colombians and said that they should therefore know all about cocaine trafficking in Mexico. The students were beaten in the van and taken to the house where one of them lived, which the police ransacked, allegedly stealing money and other valuables.

While they were there, a Mexican student came to the house and was also detained and beaten. All three were then taken to the other Colombian student's house, which was also ransacked, and two Colombian women who lived there were detained. All five were then forced into the van and driven to a car park, where their captors had to identify themselves as federal police officers to gain entry. There the Colombian students were tortured with beatings, near-suffocation and electric shocks. After this they were put back in the van and told they were going to be taken to a place the police referred to as "the canal". The students believed this to be the place in the city centre where the victims of paramilitary "death squads" were dumped during the 1970s. However, they were

MEXICO

all released a short time later after being beaten and threatened with death if they said anything about their experiences.

The whole incident lasted about four or five hours. The student interviewed by Amnesty International in May 1990 said that the police officers who had detained him and the others were in constant radio contact with other police officers. He said his hearing had been impaired as a result of being beaten around the head and that he suffered severe pain in the chest and abdomen as a result of beatings on the rest of his body. He was examined by one of Amnesty International's delegates, a medical doctor, who confirmed the existence of injuries consistent with the torture described.

All of the victims in this case decided not to make an official complaint about their treatment because of fear of reprisals: "We only want to be able to continue studying in peace", said the student interviewed by Amnesty International.

Two United States (US) citizens awaiting trial on drugs charges in Piedras Negras Prison, Coahuila state in February 1990 alleged that they were tortured following their arrest. Joe Pemberton and Henry Van Cleave were arrested by federal judicial police agents without warrants in mid-1989. Henry Van Cleave reportedly said that, although it was true that he had a marijuana "joint" in his pocket, the police started beating him and Joe Pemberton even before they had been searched. Both men claimed they were beaten and tortured by being given electric shocks after buckets of water had been thrown over them. They stated that they were forced to sign documents in Spanish which they could not understand and which they subsequently found out admitted their involvement in marijuana trafficking. They denied these charges.

Both men received medical treatment in custody. Joe Pemberton was treated for a fractured collar-bone and dislocated shoulder. Henry Van Cleave had to undergo two surgical operations because of internal infections, which a surgeon reportedly said were almost certainly caused by punches and kicks. In February 1990 a spokesperson for President Salinas told US journalists that the Attorney General had begun an investigation into the case. However, at the time of writing those responsible had not been brought to justice.

In March 1989 the Attorney General of the Federal District's Office issued instructions to the Public Ministry Agency responsible for the Federal District judicial police, about the treatment of people detained in connection with a criminal offence. The Attorney General's Office stipulated that "people who are detained in accordance with the law, because they are involved in the investigation of a particular crime, will be treated with the greatest respect and dignity". The instructions said Public Ministry Agents should avoid holding detainees in incommunicado detention. They required officials to facilitate and guarantee access to lawyers or legal representatives as soon as requested by the detainee, as long as this did not interfere with the progress of investigations. Despite these measures, torture continued to be reported in and around Mexico City.

Some seven months later, on 28 December 1989, Mario Alberto Sánchez Hinojosa, a 28-year-old mechanic, was arrested without a warrant at his workplace in Mexico City by agents of the Gustavo A. Madero unit of the Federal

CHAPTER 1

District police. For the next two days, Mario Alberto Sánchez Hinojosa was held incommunicado by the police. According to his testimony, he was tortured throughout this period with a variety of methods ranging from asphyxiation and beatings to being burned with cigarettes: 22 scars on his body apparently caused by cigarette burns were later certified by a doctor. This last form of torture was reportedly carried out by one of the senior police officers, whom Mario Alberto Sánchez Hinojosa described as "particularly sadistic".

During the torture sessions, Mario Alberto Sánchez Hinojosa learned that he was suspected of the rape and murder of his former girlfriend Rita Julieta Anguiano Torres. Under torture he confessed to the crime and on 30 December was presented at a news conference as the man responsible for the rape and murder. The following day a Mexican newspaper reported that a thorough investigation by the Federal District police, aided by forensic experts, had identified Mario Alberto Sánchez Hinojosa as the murderer of Rita Julieta Anguiano Torres. The newspaper described him as a psychopath and a sexual maniac.

Mario Alberto Sánchez Hinojosa was charged with homicide and rape and sent to the North Preventive Detention Centre in Mexico City to await trial. A few days later prison doctors carried out a routine medical examination and certified that he displayed visible signs of multiple injuries caused by a blunt object.

There were no further developments until 12 May 1990, when the Mexican press announced the arrest of gang members said to be responsible for the murder of Rita Julieta. On 16 May 1990, a senior police officer publicly announced that Mario Alberto Sánchez Hinojosa was innocent of the murder, but that he would not be released because he was still awaiting trial on charges of rape to which he had confessed. To Amnesty International's knowledge, he remains in prison awaiting trial and those responsible for the reported torture have not been brought to justice.

Police officers have also been tortured during criminal investigations. A group of Morelos state police officers arrested in February 1990 in Almoya de Juárez, Mexico state, on charges of kidnapping and extortion alleged, when brought before a judge, that they had been tortured by the Mexico state judicial police when detained. They reportedly showed the marks of torture to the judge and one of them was immediately taken to hospital because of his serious condition, said to be the result of torture. They denied the charges against them and said that they had been forced to confess under torture. They maintained that they were taken to an unofficial detention centre, where they were given electric shocks on the genitals, were half-drowned, had mineral water forced up their nostrils, were beaten about the ears with hoses, and forced to sign false statements. One of them claimed that when he refused to sign, his interrogators held a pistol to his wife's head and threatened to kill her if he did not sign. He then signed. Reportedly no one has been brought to justice as a result of their allegations.

Angel Chávez Sánchez and his 17-year-old son Alberto Chávez Barroso were abducted on 13 November 1989 in Chetumal, Quintana Roo state, by a group of

MEXICO

armed men in plain clothes who forced them into an unmarked van, and driven to the town of Cancún, a journey of approximately eight hours during which they were forced to lie on the floor of the vehicle and were reportedly beaten.

When they arrived in Cancún, Angel Chávez Sánchez and his son were hooded and taken to what they believed to be a hotel room. There they were reportedly stripped, gagged, bound and interrogated under torture about a kidnapping which had resulted in the death of the victim.

The following day, 14 November, Angel Chávez Sánchez and his son were blindfolded and taken separately to Mexico City. After arriving in Mexico City, Angel Chávez Sánchez was transferred by armed men in plain clothes to a place he later identified as the Attorney General of the Federal District's Office. There he was detained incommunicado, reportedly tortured and threatened, and forced to confess to involvement in the kidnapping. He spent a total of 20 days in incommunicado detention. On 2 December he was transferred to the North Preventive Detention Centre, in Mexico City, to await trial on charges of kidnapping and murder. The charges were reportedly based on his confession. He then learned that his son had been released without charges on 21 November.

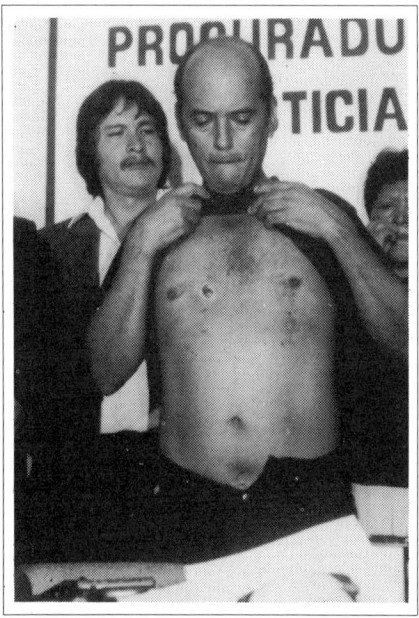

Angel Chávez Sánchez shows the wounds which he says were inflicted by torture. He says his torturers forced him to confess to a murder which he maintains he did not commit. He was charged on the basis of his confession and remanded in prison to await trial.

Angel Chávez Sánchez has repeatedly testified that he gave a false confession as a result of torture. He has presented the court with several alibis allegedly demonstrating his innocence and has also presented a complaint about what he described as his illegal detention and torture by Federal District judicial police agents. He documented the complaint with a forensic report on his wounds, the findings of which are consistent with the torture he described. He has also presented his case and that of his son to the National Human Rights Commission. However, Angel Chávez Sánchez is still in prison awaiting trial and as of May 1991 none of those allegedly responsible for the abduction and torture of him and his son have been brought to justice.

CHAPTER 1

Methods of torture

The following methods of torture are widely used in Mexico — to torture children as well as adults.

The methods are simple — crude violence, coupled with the use of simple aids, such as plastic bags, domestic mains electricity sources, and toilet bowls — but sophisticated in that they are designed to leave a minimum of marks. Sometimes they are fatal.

Beating is one of the two most common methods of torture, often starting at the moment of arrest, and most frequently reported during initial interrogation in police custody. Beating is also reported to be a common practice in several prisons throughout the country. This method includes slaps, punches and kicks to sensitive areas of the body such as the face, abdomen and genitals, blows with sticks and rifle butts, whippings with ropes and belts and twisting or pinching of the nipples.

A sophisticated variation of this method of torture is the *teléfono*, (telephone): simultaneous blows to both ears which can rupture the ear-drums and permanently damage the victim's hearing.

Many of the injuries inflicted by beatings heal without leaving permanent scars. However, victims have been permanently disabled and beatings have sometimes proved fatal. For example, Fernando Jordán de la Toba, aged 20, a suspected minor drugs trafficker, died in detention in La Paz, state of Baja California Sur, in December 1989 after being severely beaten during interrogation by the judicial police. He had been detained two days earlier. Two judicial police officers were arrested and charged in connection with his death but had not been brought to trial at the time of writing, May 1991.

The torture method known as *Tehuacanazo* takes its name from *Tehuacán* - a popular brand of carbonated mineral water. It is the second most widely reported form of torture in Mexico.

Tehuacanazo consists of the forcible introduction of carbonated water, usually mixed with hot chili powder, into the victim's nostrils, producing an extremely painful irritation of the nasal passages and difficulty in breathing. In a variation of this technique tap water is forced up the victim's nose with a hose.

Asphyxiation is a very common method of torture and can be fatal. There are two main techniques. In *la bolsita* (the bag), also known as *submarino seco* (dry submarine), a plastic bag is pulled over the victim's head and tied around the neck, causing suffocation. Sometimes the victim's head is first wrapped in a wet cloth, or hot chilies are put into the bag. The victim's distress is exacerbated by blows to the abdomen. *El pozole, pozoleado*, also know as *submarino húmedo* (wet submarine), causes asphyxiation by submerging the victim's head in water, often containing debris and sometimes faeces and urine when toilets are used. Irritants such as hot chili powder or chlorine are sometimes added to the water.

Electric torture is widely used in Mexico. It is commonly applied with an electric prod, *la chicharra* (buzzer), to sensitive parts of the body such as the eyes, gums, tongue, nipples and genitals, or in some cases by cables from an

MEXICO

electrical source, usually attached to the victim's feet and/or hands. Sometimes, electricity has been applied directly from normal household sources such as light bulb sockets.

The intensity of electric torture is often increased by throwing water over the victims or holding them down in a water container. The medical effects of this torture method include: acute pain, convulsions, multiple trauma, burns and cardiac arrest.

Interrogation sessions frequently have been accompanied by intimidation and threats of different kinds. Detainees have often been told by their interrogators that they will "disappear", or be killed, if they do not cooperate. Sometimes they are threatened with reprisals against relatives — the rape of their daughters or the killing of their children. Antonio Orozco Michel, one of several people arrested and charged with bank raids on behalf of a guerrilla left-wing organization, made an official complaint that he was tortured during his interrogation. In his testimony he describes being told by the head of the police that "they had orders to blow our brains out if we persisted in our denials". Other forms of reported psychological torture include mock executions.

Another form of torture entails the application of lighted cigarettes to the skin of the victim, producing painful burns. One victim was medically certified to have 22 such burns.

Although sexual abuse is not a widely reported method of torture during interrogation of detainees, there are reports of women being threatened with rape and stripped in custody. Guards in some prisons have been allegedly responsible for sporadic cases of rape and sexual abuse against male and female prisoners. Sexual abuse has also been reported in rural areas. Three women among 113 people detained on 24 January 1990 at El Caracol Bridge, Tuxtepec, Oaxaca state, on their way to a demonstration in the state capital city alleged that they were sexually abused by the state police while in detention and forced to sign confessions.

Another torture technique, *Pollo rostizado*, also known as the parrot perch, involves hanging the victim for prolonged periods of time from a metal or wooden bar. The wrists and ankles are tied together, the knees are bent and the victim is suspended from a bar inserted between the knees and arms causing excruciating pain and injury to muscles, tendons, and joints. A reported variation of this method consists of hanging the handcuffed victim by the wrists so that his or her feet barely touch the ground. This creates similar strains on the wrists.

In *antorcha* (the torch), a flame is applied directly to the victim's skin with burning paper, cigarette lighters, welding torches and other devices.

The various methods of torture described have reportedly often been used in combination, the most common being the practice of beatings together with or followed by *tehuacanazo, la bolsita*, electric shocks, and psychological torture.

2

Torture: the legal context

Torture is prohibited by the Constitution of Mexico. Mexico has ratified international human rights treaties which prohibit torture and require the government to take effective measures to prevent it. Further legislation to prevent torture and to punish its perpetrators has been adopted by the federal government and several Mexican states. Government officials have frequently made statements condemning torture and calling for investigations and prosecutions in cases of torture to be conducted in accordance with the law. An official body charged with investigating complaints of torture has been established at national level and similar bodies exist in some Mexican states.

Despite this, human rights abuses by law enforcement agents continue to be reported throughout Mexico and those allegedly responsible are rarely brought to justice.

Legal prohibition of torture

The Constitution of the Republic of Mexico, proclaimed in 1917, guarantees the protection of a series of basic rights. No one may be arrested without a warrant issued by a competent judicial authority, except when caught in the act of committing a crime *(flagrante delicto)*. No one may be compelled to testify against themselves. All forms of ill-treatment during detention are prohibited. All detainees must be brought before a judge within 24 hours of arrest and they have the right to legal counsel from the moment of arrest.

The Mexican Government is also obliged to protect human rights by the international treaties it has ratified, among them the International Covenant on Civil and Political Rights[1], the American Convention on

---

1   Mexico has still not ratified the (First) Optional Protocol of the Covenant which enables individuals to submit a written complaint to the United Nations Human Rights Committee alleging that their rights under the Covenant have been violated.

MEXICO

Human Rights[2], and the UN Convention against Torture and Other Cruel, Inhuman or Degrading Treatment or Punishment[3].

In May 1986 Congress approved the Federal Law to Prevent and Punish Torture. The seven articles of this law include: a legal definition of torture as a crime for which prosecution is mandatory irrespective of whether individual complaints have been made; the recognition of detainees' rights to proper medical care or examination by a doctor of their choice on request; a prohibition on the use in legal proceedings of evidence based on confessions obtained under torture; and the provision of penalties for law enforcement agents found guilty of torture of up to eight years' imprisonment plus dismissal from duties for double the prison sentence. This law also expressly states that no special circumstances or public emergency of any kind can be invoked to justify torture.

In February 1991 a series of reforms were introduced to the Federal Code of Penal Proceedings and to the Penal Code for the Federal District: the new measures limit the role of the police in questioning defendants, provide interpreters for non-Spanish speaking defendants and reinforce the prohibition of arbitrary arrest and incommunicado detention, as well as any form of abuse or intimidation against detainees. The reforms also include provisions to limit the value of confessions as evidence in courts by stipulating that confessions by defendants should be accompanied by additional evidence to substantiate charges and that statements by defendants are to be considered valid only when made before the Public Ministry or the courts and in the presence of a defence counsel.

Although Amnesty International welcomes the adoption of these reforms, the organization is concerned that some of the new measures may in practice be inadequate in preventing torture or ill-treatment. For example, the requirement that confessions should only be considered valid when presented before a Public Ministry Agent or the courts may not prevent defendants from being coerced into making confessions before such officials because, during the first stages of their

---

2   Mexico has still not made a declaration recognizing as binding the jurisdiction of the Inter-American Court of Human Rights (on all matters relating to the interpretation or application of the American Convention).

3   Mexico has not yet made a declaration under Article 22 of the Convention, and therefore has not recognized the competence of the Committee against Torture to receive and examine complaints from or on behalf of individuals who claim to be victims of violations of the Convention.

detention, the police had tortured them or threatened reprisals against them or their relatives unless they confessed. Nor does it address the frequently reported role of Public Ministry Agents in condoning the torture or ill-treatment of detainees.

These are the latest of a series of legal and administrative reforms adopted by the Mexican Government with the stated intention of curbing the practice of torture and ill-treatment. Despite reforms in the past intended to prevent such abuses, Amnesty International continued to receive a great number of reports of torture and ill-treatment.

There is also legislation at state level designed to prevent and punish torture. In May 1990 the state of Sinaloa incorporated anti-torture legislation into its penal code with a penalty of between two and 10 years' imprisonment for those found responsible. This legislation appeared to have been approved partly as the result of initiatives undertaken by human rights lawyer Norma Corona Sapién. Other Mexican states which have adopted anti-torture legislation in the past include Querétaro, Chihuahua and Aguascalientes.

In addition, some Mexican states have created government offices specifically responsible for human rights issues, among them the Attorney for the Defence of Indigenous Peoples in Oaxaca; the Attorney in charge of Social Affairs of the Mountainous Region in Guerrero; the Commission of Human Rights in Morelos; the State Attorney for Citizen Protection — a State Ombudsman position — and the State Human Rights Commission in Aguascalientes; and the Federal District's Attorney for Social Affairs.

Official response to torture

Public concern over the increasing number of torture cases reported in Mexico has prompted both national and state officials to make a series of statements apparently intended to stop the use of torture and to reinforce the basic rights to which all citizens are entitled.

In February 1989 the General Human Rights Directorate was set up within the Interior Ministry. One of its main designated functions was to receive complaints of human rights abuses and to make recommendations for their investigation and prevention to the relevant authorities. Its Director General, Luis Ortiz Monasterio, and several other officials subsequently acknowledged that torture occurred in Mexico but denied that it was a deliberate policy. They criticized the use of confessions taken by police as evidence of high probatory value against defendants because of the risk that the confessions might have been obtained through coercion.

At a national level, following continuing public complaints about torture by the federal judicial police, the Republic Attorney General in mid-1989 promised a full investigation into allegations that federal judicial police agents were responsible for torture and that the full weight of the law would be brought to bear on anyone found guilty of such acts. A few months later, local councillors complained to the Republic Attorney General about arbitrary detentions carried

MEXICO

out in Mexico City by the federal judicial police, saying they had received complaints that men and women were being arbitrarily detained, for periods of from four to 12 days without being brought before a judge, whereas the maximum period stipulated by the Constitution is 24 hours. It is during such periods of incommunicado detention that torture is most likely to occur.

In January 1990 the Federal District Attorney General announced further measures to be taken in response to concern over reports of torture and ill-treatment in the Federal District. He stated that convictions could no longer be based on extrajudicial confessions alone; other evidence of guilt would have to be presented by the prosecution. He also stipulated that before and after interrogation, detainees must be examined by the medical service of the Public Ministry Agent. Detainees should be informed of their right to appoint a defence lawyer and the lawyer may be present during questioning. People detained by the police while committing a crime should immediately be transferred to the custody of the Public Ministry. He also said that at all times, the police should act only on the orders of the authority of the Public Ministry. Any official found guilty of torture or using coercion to obtain a confession would face between two and 10 years' imprisonment.

The Federal District Attorney General's statements did not stop reports of torture and illegal detentions by law enforcement agents in and around the Federal District. On 22 August 1990 he announced further measures, which included the stipulation that the police could only interrogate criminal defendants in the presence of the Public Ministry Agent, and a request to Public Ministry Agents in the Federal District to avoid charging detainees with criminal offences solely on the basis of their confessions.

The experience at national and Federal District level — that official prohibition has failed to curb the use of torture — has been reflected at state level. State governors have on several occasions expressed condemnation of torture and ill-treatment, and sometimes promised prosecution of police officers found responsible for these abuses, but this has failed to stop torture.

The National Human Rights Commission

In June 1990 the government took a national initiative over the issue of human rights abuse in Mexico. Shortly after Norma Corona Sapién's murder, President Salinas announced the creation of the National Human Rights Commission, to be chaired by Jorge Carpizo McGregor, once a member of the Supreme Court and former rector of the National Autonomous University of Mexico. The commission was created by presidential decree and is a part of the Interior Ministry. The General Human Rights Directorate created in 1989 was incorporated into the commission as its technical secretariat. At the commission's inaugural ceremony on 6 June 1990 President Salinas proclaimed: "Things are going to change in Mexico. We shall confront the new threats to human rights from wherever they come. The new social will and the aim of the reformed State is to adhere to the law...Let there be no doubt: the political line of the government of the Republic is to defend human rights and punish those who violate them; it is to end once and for all any kind of impunity. Mexico, the government, does not condone any violation of the guarantees enshrined in the Constitution."

The National Human Rights Commission's main function is to receive and investigate complaints of human rights abuses and to make recommendations for action based on its findings to the relevant authorities. However, it has been given neither the broad investigative powers nor the constitutional authority to carry out these tasks effectively. The commission is also responsible for human rights promotion and education in Mexico, and for proposing a national policy for the respect and defence of human rights. In addition, it is responsible for presenting the government's human rights policy at national and international level. The commission reports twice a year on its activities and findings with corresponding recommendations. It issued its first report to the authorities in December 1990.

Most independent human rights organizations in Mexico welcomed the creation of the commission. However, they publicly expressed concern that it was not an independent body and that it did not have full investigatory powers. Many believed that the commission's independence and authority, and therefore its effectiveness, would have been greater had its creation been debated and approved in Congress, rather than instituted by presidential decree.

Nearly one year later, in May 1991, these concerns continued to be voiced following the outcome of some of the investigations undertaken by the commission. In its first bi-annual report, presented six months after its formation, the commission reported that it had collected information on over 1,000 complaints of torture and recommended prosecution in 33 cases. In not one of these cases have convictions been obtained, even when the commission's investigations yielded substantial evidence of the involvement of individual police officers in torture, ill-treatment and other human rights violations. Most of the commission's recommendations have not been implemented by the Republic Attorney General.

The new commission's first major task was to investigate the murder of Norma Corona Sapién. In July 1990 it was announced that five individuals had been arrested in connection with the case. Three were civilians. The other two were former federal judicial police officers, one of whom had confessed to having carried out her killing on the orders of a senior officer who had been killed in unclear circumstances at the end of June. However, he later retracted his confession, alleging that he had given it under torture. As of May 1991 there had been no further progress in the case reported, despite widespread public demand for full investigations.

In dozens of cases the commission's investigations have resulted in well-documented accounts of human rights abuses, many of which were cases of torture. But its recommendations for the investigation of these cases and the prosecution of those responsible have rarely been acted on, and the commission has no authority to force them to be considered.

MEXICO

Soon after the commission was set up it was presented with allegations of torture by Antonio Francisco Valencia Fontes, a lawyer from Ciudad Obregón in Sonora state. The case concerned the lawyer, his client Jesús Enrique Machi Ramírez, his client's brother Sergio Machi Ramírez, and another relative. Sergio Machi Ramírez "disappeared" and was later found dead; the other three are in prison awaiting trial on drugs charges.

Sergio Machi Ramírez was last seen alive in federal judicial police custody. Three days later his body was found, handcuffed and charred beyond immediate recognition. Those allegedly responsible have not been brought to justice.

Sergio Machi Ramírez "disappeared" on 19 November 1989 after being detained by the federal police in Mexicali, Baja California Norte state. Two days later, on 21 November, Antonio Francisco Valencia Fontes and Jesús Enrique Machi Ramírez flew from Ciudad Obregón to Mexicali to try to establish Sergio Machi Ramírez's whereabouts. In Mexicali the two men were joined by Armando Machi Bustamante, a relative of Jesús Enrique Machi Ramírez, and together they visited several police stations to make inquiries. That night the hotel where they were staying was raided by a federal judicial police anti-narcotics squad and the three men were taken to the police headquarters. There, according to their testimonies, they were beaten, subjected to electric torture and to near-asphyxiation by having plastic bags containing ammonia placed over their heads, subjected to mock executions and threatened. They also claimed that they had seen Sergio Machi Ramírez in the police station and that he appeared to have been tortured.

The following day Antonio Francisco Valencia Fontes, Jesús Enrique Machi Ramírez and Armando Machi Bustamante were transferred, handcuffed and blindfold, to a cell at the Republic Attorney General's Office in Mexico City where, they claimed, they were tortured and forced to confess to possessing cocaine. On 29 November, at 1am, they were transferred to the East Preventive Detention Centre, to await trial.

On 17 January 1990 the three men presented a formal complaint of unjustified arrest to the President of the Mexican Supreme Court of Justice. Their complaint was supported by several organizations, including the Sonora state Bar Association. It documented 10 contradictions between events described in their formal complaint and the police version of what had occurred.

In August the National Human Rights Commission concluded its investigations into the case with the finding that there were "irregularities in the proceedings...which would give weight to Lic. Valencia's declarations...that he is not responsible for the drug charges of which he has been accused". Prominent among the irregularities was the fact that according to the arrest warrants issued by the Attorney General's Office, Jesús Enrique Machi Ramírez, Antonio Valencia Fontes and Armando Machi Bustamante were all arrested on 27 November in Mexicali in possession of almost a kilo of cocaine, whereas the commission had proved the men were already in detention in Mexico City on that date.

The commission recommended that the Republic Attorney General conduct a thorough investigation into the irregularities in the case and review the detainees' legal situation. It also recommended that the Attorney General should publish the findings. None of the recommendations were accepted. Instead the Attorney General confirmed the charges against Antonio Francisco Valencia Fontes, Jesús Enrique Machi Ramírez and Armando Machi Bustamante. In September the commission requested that the Attorney General release Antonio Francisco Valencia Fontes without charge on the grounds that his constitutional guarantees had been violated. This request was also rejected. Antonio Francisco Valencia Fontes, Jesús Enrique Machi Ramírez and Armando Machi Bustamante were still in detention awaiting trial at the time of writing, May 1991.

The whereabouts of Sergio Machi Ramírez remained unknown until November 1990. Three days after his brother and his lawyer claimed to have seen him alive in custody, the remains of a partially charred body, handcuffed and with a bullet wound in the skull, were found in La Rumorosa, on the outskirts of Mexicali. It took almost a year for forensic scientists to confirm that the remains were those of Sergio Machi Ramírez. A 45 calibre bullet was reportedly found at the scene of the crime, but no ballistic examination is known to have been carried out. Nor has there been any attempt to establish the origin of the handcuffs, although they are reported to be similar to those used by law enforcement agents.

On 15 March 1991 the commission published the results of its investigation of the "disappearance" and killing of Sergio Machi Ramírez. The commission had established that he was detained in Mexicali by the federal judicial police on 19 November 1989 and transferred to their local headquarters, where he was held incommunicado and tortured before being transferred again on or around 23 November, the day he was last seen alive, to an unknown destination. The commission interviewed several former detainees who had seen Sergio Machi Ramírez in the federal police headquarters. They alleged that he had been brutally tortured with beatings, near-asphyxiation with water and plastic bags, and that a hose had been introduced into his rectum and water pumped into his intestines. The commission recommended to the state governor and the Republic Attorney General's Office that those alleged to be responsible be suspended from duty and brought to justice. However, as of May 1991 no action is known to have been taken in response to these recommendations.

Another well-known case in which the commission's recommendations for investigation and prosecution were not acted on, concerns the killings, widely

MEXICO

believed to have been extrajudicial executions, of three brothers in January 1990, one of whom had first been brutally tortured.

The first arrests in the case were made on 12 January 1990 in Ciudad Juárez, Chihuahua state. Two of the brothers, Héctor Ignacio and Sergio Máximo Quijano Santoyo, were detained by federal judicial police in connection with an anti-narcotics investigation. The following day their father, Francisco Quijano García, was arrested by federal police agents in the bar that he ran in Mexico City. Shortly after his arrest, another of his sons, former police officer Francisco Flavio Quijano Santoyo, who had gone to visit his father, was involved in a gunfight outside the bar with police officers and a *madrina*. Apparently they stopped him at gunpoint without identifying themselves. He thought they were going to assault him, snatched a pistol from one of them, and a gun battle ensued in which two federal police officers were killed.

Francisco Flavio Quijano managed to escape and his father, by now in custody in the headquarters of the Republic Attorney General's Office, was interrogated reportedly under torture about his son's whereabouts and forced to identify his house in Mexico state. The torture he described consisted of beatings, near-asphyxiation and forcing carbonated water up his nostrils. Francisco Quijano García later claimed that on the day of his arrest he saw in detention one of his two sons arrested in Ciudad Juárez, Héctor Ignacio Quijano Santoyo, and that he had been severely tortured.

The following day, 14 January, an anti-narcotics squad of some 50 federal police officers in vehicles and helicopters surrounded the house of Francisco Quijano García's ex-wife in Ojo de Agua, Mexico state, in pursuit of his fugitive son. They had brought Héctor Ignacio Quijano Santoyo with them. Francisco Flavio Quijano Santoyo was not there but two other brothers, Jaime Mauro Quijano Santoyo and Erik Dante Quijano Santoyo, came out of the house with their hands up. According to statements from other members of the family and reports from eye-witnesses, one brother was forced to kneel and was then shot in the back at close range, and the other was shot dead while he had his hands up. The police then raided the house and arrested the women, and the children who were all under 10 years old. Héctor Ignacio Quijano Santoyo was taken into the house and shot dead. The women and children were taken back to the Republic Attorney General's Office in Mexico City and held until 18 January, when they were released without charge.

On 19 January 1990 Francisco Quijano García, who had effectively "disappeared" for six days, was released without charge. He immediately presented formal complaints to the authorities about the deaths of his three sons, but not about his own detention and torture. The case gained widespread publicity in the press.

The police claimed that the Quijano Santoyo brothers had been killed in an armed confrontation, but eye-witness and other evidence disputed this claim (see page 41). Eye-witnesses claimed that the men had been unarmed and photographic evidence suggested that the police altered the scene of the killings to conform with their account of events. One year after the incident, in January

CHAPTER 2

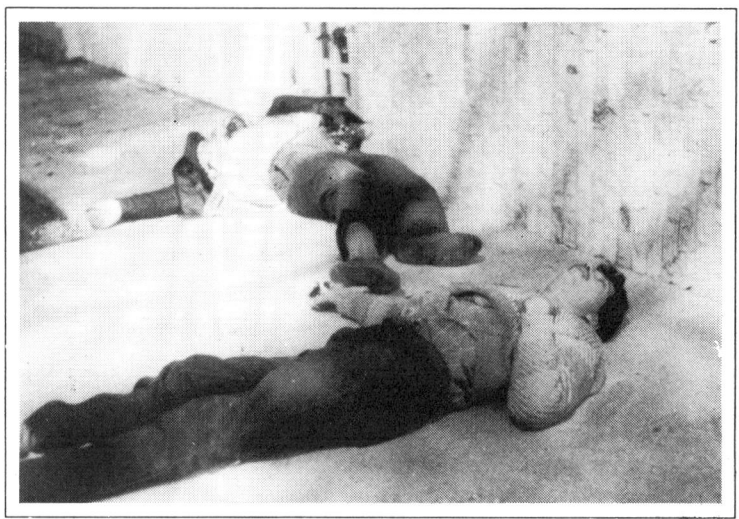

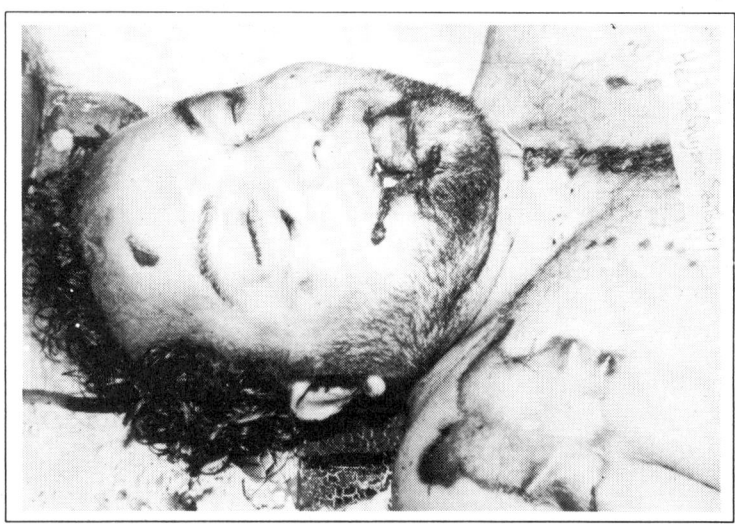

Erik Dante Quijano Santoyo and Jaime Mauro Quijano Santoyo were shot dead by the police. Both men reportedly were unarmed and had given themselves up. (Below) Their brother, Héctor Ignacio Quijano Santoyo, shown here in an autopsy photograph, was killed at the same time. He had been detained several days earlier, and reportedly brutally tortured; independent forensic examination noted injuries consistent with beatings and burns.

MEXICO

1991, the National Human Rights Commission recommended that the Republic Attorney General carry out a full investigation into the killing of Erik Dante, Jaime Mauro and Héctor Ignacio Quijano Santoyo. It also recommended that the police officers involved in the killings should be suspended from duty during the investigation. As of May 1991 the Attorney General had not responded.

Between January and June 1990, Francisco Quijano García continued to campaign for an investigation into the killing of his sons. He reported receiving death threats both by telephone and from individuals who stopped him in the street. On 17 June his daughter, Rosalba Quijano Santoyo, said she had received anonymous telephone calls threatening her with death if the family continued to publicize the case.

Francisco Quijano García "disappeared" four days later, on 21 June, from his house in Mexico City. The case was taken to the National Human Rights Commission which agreed to investigate reports that he was in detention and requested permission to search for him at the headquarters of the Attorney General's Office. This request was granted but the commission was given only limited access to the building and was thus unable to conduct a complete search. The commission's president, Dr Jorge Carpizo, then contacted the Attorney General who apparently told him that Francisco Quijano was not in detention and suggested that he might have gone abroad to meet his fugitive son.

After Francisco Quijano García "disappeared", his daughter presented to the judicial authorities formal complaints that he had been abducted.

In March 1991 the Federal District General Attorney's Office announced that Francisco Quijano García's body had been found. The announcement stated that he had been killed on the day he "disappeared" by a partner who had been arrested on 12 March 1991 and had confessed to the murder. However, two days later this individual claimed before a judge that his confession had been obtained under duress. Francisco Quijano García's relatives have continued to call for further investigations into the alleged participation of federal judicial police agents in his abduction and murder.

The surviving brother in this case, Sergio Máximo Quijano Santoyo, is still in detention awaiting trial, in a Mexico City prison. According to reports he had also been tortured after he had been detained and following his transferral to prison with beatings, near-asphyxiation and *tehuacanazo*.

3

Factors facilitating torture

The principal factors which facilitate the practice of torture by law enforcement agents in Mexico are: constitutional safeguards are routinely violated; aspects of the Mexican criminal justice system foster the use of torture; investigation and prosecution of the perpetrators is rare and the victims of torture and their relatives are provided with few and inadequate means of seeking redress.

Mexican jurisprudence, criminal law and legal procedure

Certain aspects of Mexican jurisprudence, criminal law and legal procedures appear to facilitate torture by law enforcement agents.

Under the Mexican Constitution the Public Ministry is responsible for both investigating and prosecuting before the courts crimes under its jurisdiction; requesting arrest warrants; procuring and presenting evidence against suspects; ensuring that trials are conducted in accordance with the law; and requesting the imposition of sentence.

The Public Ministry Agent is a prosecutor responsible to the state Attorney General's Office for the investigation and prosecution of offences under the state penal code, and to the Republic Attorney General for the prosecution of federal offences. The federal and state judicial police forces, most frequently cited in reports of torture, are an auxiliary body of the Public Ministry and operate under its direction. The Republic Attorney General's Office, which is responsible to the executive power, is the ultimate supervisory body of all federal Public Ministry Agents in the country, as are the Federal District General Attorney and each of the states Attorneys General responsible for the Public Ministry under their jurisdiction.

The combination of the prosecutory and investigative powers under the authority of the Public Ministry Agent coupled with the frequent practice by police under the Public Ministry's supervision of using confessions to substantiate criminal charges, appears to facilitate the use of torture.

Constitutional safeguards prohibiting arbitrary arrest and incommunicado detention are routinely violated. The Mexican Constitution permits detentions without an

MEXICO

arrest warrant only in cases of *flagrante delicto* and then stipulates that the detainee must be immediately brought before a judge. However, arrests without warrants are a common and widely tolerated practice.

Similarly, incommunicado detention is routine during the initial stages of detention and interrogation — the period when torture most commonly occurs — despite the fact that the Mexican Constitution explicitly forbids incommunicado detention. Under the Constitution, a detainee has the right to legal counsel from the moment of detention and must be brought before a judge within 24 hours, a period during which the detainee is in the custody of the Public Ministry Agent. According to Mexican law, the maximum period of pre-judicial detention should not exceed 24 hours from the moment the suspect is arrested until his or her presentation before a judge. The judge should then decide, after hearing the detainee's preliminary declaration, whether to release, charge and/or remand the detainee within a maximum period of 48 hours. No one should be held for more than three days without a formal detention order issued by a judge. These provisions are rarely respected and the stipulation that detention by the Public Ministry Agent cannot exceed 24 hours is the most frequently flouted.

One of the principal aspects of the Mexican criminal justice system which encourages torture and ill-treatment is the continuing acceptance of confessions obtained under duress during initial interrogation often as the sole evidence on which defendants are convicted, despite the fact that the Constitution, other Mexican legislation and international standards specifically prohibit forcing a defendant to testify against him or herself.

These confessions are obtained during preliminary investigation when the defendant is in the custody of the police or the Public Ministry Agent. During this period, detainees rarely have access to a lawyer (or a translator for non-Spanish speakers). These confessions are given legal precedence over subsequent contradictory statements a defendant may make, even in cases where he or she claims that the first confession was made under torture.

In addition, the Supreme Court has ruled in the past that once a confession has been given, the onus is on the defendant to prove that it was illegally obtained if it is to be ruled out of evidence. However, medical evidence produced by defendants in support of torture allegations has routinely been dismissed by the courts. This seriously undermines guarantees and rights of victims enshrined in the Constitution and in the UN Convention against Torture and Other Cruel, Inhuman or Degrading Treatment or Punishment. It is also in violation of Mexico's obligations under the UN Convention against Torture to investigate thoroughly all allegations of torture presented by defendants and to dismiss from court any confession obtained under torture, except when submitted as evidence of the crime of torture.

In one well-known case a defendant, whose claim that he had confessed under torture — supported by a medical report — was dismissed by the court, later died apparently as a result of internal injuries sustained under torture. Rubén Oropeza Hurtado, aged 40, was arrested without a warrant on 29 March 1990 by the federal judicial police in Tijuana, Baja California Norte state. He was illegally

CHAPTER 3

held incommunicado until 6 April, several days in excess of the maximum period of pre-judicial detention allowed, when he was brought to court by the Public Ministry Agent on charges of possessing drugs to which he had confessed in detention. In his preliminary statement to the judge, Rubén Oropeza Hurtado denied the charges and said that he had confessed because he was severely tortured by police officers and *madrinas*. His confession was the only evidence against him. The court ordered a routine medical examination and the doctor's report found some external injuries consistent with the allegation of torture.

Rubén Oropeza Hurtado died in hospital apparently as a result of abdominal injuries caused by torture. Those responsible have not been brought to justice.

Despite this the judge upheld the charges and ordered Rubén Oropeza Hurtado to be detained pending trial. He was transferred to *La Mesa* State Penitentiary in Tijuana, but did not receive adequate medical treatment for his injuries and, according to other detainees, was constantly in pain. At the end of June he joined 60 fellow inmates of *La Mesa* in a hunger-strike, protesting against unjust trials and convictions based on confessions extracted under torture.

On 14 July Rubén Oropeza Hurtado was taken to the emergency ward of the local Red Cross Clinic, in great pain and in a very critical condition. That day he underwent major surgery which included the removal of a great part of his intestines. According to the doctors, he had developed a complicated hernia, caused by a recent violent blow which had ruptured his diaphragm. His post-operative condition was described as critical: his survival depended on permanent intravenous feeding and complex medical treatment, facilities unavailable in the Red Cross clinic. His transfer to a hospital which could provide adequate treatment was considered urgent. Local human rights organizations campaigned for him to be given the necessary medical treatment and won national publicity for his case. They also took the case to the National Human Rights Commission. One month later, on 15 August, Rubén Oropeza Hurtado was transferred to the intensive care unit of the General Hospital of the Mexican Social Health Care Institute, in Tijuana. His medical condition continued to be critical.

On 29 August the National Human Rights Commission concluded its investigation of the case with the findings that Rubén Oropeza Hurtado had suffered torture following arrest and had been forced to confess under duress. The commission recommended that the Attorney General's Office immediately

MEXICO

suspend from duty the police officers involved in Rubén Oropeza Hurtado's arrest and torture; and initiate criminal proceeding against them, the *madrinas* who participated in the torture, and the senior officers in charge of the case.

Rubén Oropeza Hurtado died while still in custody on 1 October at 3.15am. According to the death certificate issued by a forensic doctor, the cause of death was malnutrition secondary to generalized infection. His body was cremated two days later, allegedly without the consent of his wife. At the time of writing, May 1991, the Attorney General's Office had taken no action on the commission's recommendations. Those believed to be responsible have not been brought to justice nor have they been suspended from their duties.

In many cases of death in custody where torture was alleged, routine autopsies have failed to adequately diagnose and document human rights abuses. These autopsies are carried out by forensic doctors working for the Public Ministry medical service. In contentious cases, their findings have tended to corroborate the police version of events.

Five days after he had been taken into custody by state police agents, the relatives of Jesús Manuel Martínez Ruiz found his body buried in a common grave in a local cemetery in Villahermosa, Tabasco state. They were told by a cemetery official that the body had been brought there by state police officers on 5 September, the day after Jesús Manuel Martínez Ruiz and three others had been detained in a Villahermosa suburb.

The state police eventually admitted that Jesús Manuel Martínez Ruiz had died in custody, but claimed that he had been drunk when arrested and had choked to death on his own vomit. In support of this they produced the report of an autopsy performed by forensic doctors of the Public Ministry medical service. The relatives' request that the body be exhumed for a second autopsy was initially rejected.

One of the three other men who had been detained at the same time and subsequently released without charge, Julio César Márquez Valenzuela, gave a very different account of how Jesús Manuel Martínez Ruiz died. He said that after he, Jesús Manuel Martínez Ruiz and the two others had been arrested the police took them to a nearby deserted beach in Centla, known as Miramar, and tortured them with kicks, beatings, electric shocks and near-asphyxiation by submersion in the sea, and that this last method of torture had killed Jesús Manuel Martínez Ruiz. His allegations were later supported by one of the police officers involved in arresting the men.

Julio César Márquez Valenzuela claimed that if a second autopsy was performed it would reveal that Jesús Manuel Martínez Ruiz had drowned. He told journalists that he intended to present his testimony to the General Human Rights Directorate (predecessor of the National Human Rights Commission), and accused the state Attorney General and the state judicial police chief of covering up the crime.

In 13 October 1989 Julio César Márquez Valenzuela was rearrested in Villahermosa by the state police and allegedly forced to confess to several charges including two of murder. He was then transferred to the Tabasco state prison in

CHAPTER 3

Villahermosa to await trial. That same month the relatives of Jesús Manuel Martínez Ruiz reported that they were being threatened by state judicial police.

On 24 October the state Attorney General agreed to the exhumation of the body for a second autopsy, and said that this could be carried out by independent doctors if the family wished. The second autopsy, carried out on 7 November, was performed by doctors appointed by state and federal authorities — the Ministry of Public Health, the Tabasco Medical Association, the Attorney General's Office and the General Human Rights Directorate. It concluded that the body "shows no indications that could alter the result of the first autopsy". However, contrary to legal requirements, both the heart and the lungs were found to have been removed during the first autopsy, making it impossible to determine the exact cause of death. At the family's request, the General Human Rights Directorate requested further laboratory analysis of some parts of the body, but the state authorities declared that there was no crime to pursue and declared the case closed.

This case was taken up again, some months later, by the National Human Rights Commission. In September 1990 the commission issued a series of recommendations to the Tabasco state governor. These included re-opening investigations into the killing of Jesús Manuel Martínez Ruíz; dismissing from duty and bringing to justice any law enforcement personnel involved; and providing protection for the victim's relatives and witnesses, who had received threats. The commission's recommendations have been largely ignored. Julio César Márquez Valenzuela remains in prison awaiting trial and has allegedly received death threats because of his testimony.

A similar pattern — where inadequate autopsies carried out by the Public Ministry medical service have substantiated the police version of events — can be seen in other cases. In the case of the three Quijano Santoyo brothers killed in January 1990, the federal judicial police claimed that they had been killed in an armed confrontation, and that all three had been wearing bullet-proof jackets. The findings of the autopsies carried out by the Federal District Medical Examiner's Office did not dispute this version of events. Amnesty International obtained copies of the autopsy reports and photographs of the bodies and sent them to the Cook County Institute of Forensic Medicine in Chicago, USA, for analysis. The institute found: "The distribution and trajectory of the gunshot injuries is consistent with execution-style slayings and highly unlikely to be the result of injuries sustained in a shoot-out". The institute also found discrepancies in the autopsy report on Héctor Ignacio Quijano Santoyo, in that the report made no reference to injuries sustained prior to his death which are clearly discernable in a photograph of his body attached to the report — injuries such as "blunt trauma injuries to the face and unexplained injuries to the chest, consistent with burns".

The Public Ministry rarely provides adequate medical treatment to those detainees who allege they have been tortured, even in cases where there are evident signs and symptoms of torture. In one case a detainee died in custody

MEXICO

shortly after being examined by two forensic doctors who concluded he had no life-threatening injuries.

Immunity from prosecution

A principal factor why torture is widespread is the almost total impunity extended to the torturers. Police officers implicated are rarely subject to an investigation and even less frequently prosecuted. In October 1990 Jorge Carpizo, President of the National Human Rights Commission acknowledged the problem in a public statement: "Police officers who engage in torture are neither sadists nor deranged, they are convinced that they are doing their duty. They know that in most cases, even when they exceed themselves to the point of homicide, they won't be punished because their chiefs will defend or cover up for them..."

In September 1990 Javier Coello Trejo, the Deputy Attorney General in charge of anti-narcotics investigations, responded to growing criticism of human rights violations by the federal narcotics agents under his command by asserting that drug wars had to be fought with an iron fist and that drug-traffickers, when they were caught, could not be "collared with caresses"[1]. He had earlier become the target of criticism when two of his personal bodyguards were formally charged in March 1990 with participating in a series of rapes in Mexico City.

In mid-October 1990 Javier Coello Trejo was relieved of his responsibility for anti-narcotics investigations and promoted to the post of Federal Attorney for the Consumer. His former office was dissolved and replaced by the General Coordination Office for Anti-narcotics Investigations. One of the duties of this office, according to the government, was to prevent human rights violations during anti-narcotics investigations, but reports of torture and other abuses by anti-narcotics agents continued thereafter.

Human rights monitors in Mexico have called for an investigation into repeated charges that federal judicial police agents under Javier Coello Trejo's command had committed widespread human rights abuses because, as María Teresa Jardí, a lawyer for the independent Human Rights and Solidarity Commission, put it: "Crimes must not remain unpunished. Impunity should not prevail, because everybody in the public service including the President of the Republic would become accomplices". However, despite their efforts, impunity continues to prevail.

Relatively few of the hundreds of reported cases of torture, sometimes resulting

---

1   *Reuters*, 30 September 1990

CHAPTER 3

in death, many of which are well-documented and publicized, have been investigated by the courts.

Complaints of torture are often difficult to prove since torture most frequently occurs while detainees are held incommunicado by the police, without access to lawyers, doctors or relatives and therefore unable to produce witnesses to support their claims. In addition, many of the techniques used to torture detainees are designed to leave no marks. Even in cases where medical or other testimonial evidence supports the detainees' allegations of torture, judges have often decided that this has no bearing on detainees' confessions, and have refused to open investigations into the allegations.

In February 1990 Carlos Gilberto Morán Cortéz, former president of the "Eustaquio Buelna" Lawyers Association, Sinaloa state, sought publicity for a case in which two mentally retarded detainees, arrested by state police in Zapote de los Cazarez, Mocorito, were allegedly held incommunicado for three days and tortured with electric shocks. The judge before whom the case was brought refused to admit as evidence medical certificates relating to the torture. The detainees' lawyer subsequently presented a formal complaint to the Public Ministry but no action was taken.

A few days later, in response to publicity about the case, the President of the Supreme Court of Justice of Sinaloa urged criminal defendants in police custody to present evidence of any torture they might have suffered. He said that judges were obliged to admit evidence of ill-treatment and torture, and to review any confessions which might have been made under duress as well as to prosecute those responsible. He stated that torture could not be tolerated.

On 10 February 1990 Jorge Juárez Paz, a 55-year-old fisherman, died in custody in the municipal prison in Himanquillo, Tabasco state. He was reportedly detained the night before and beaten to death in the prison by police officers. The death certificate issued by the state Attorney General's office said that he had died from acute cardio-respiratory arrest. The Tabasco Human Rights Committee made a formal complaint that Jorge Juárez Paz was killed by police officers but to Amnesty International's knowledge his complaint reportedly has not been investigated.

In April 1990 Amnesty International received reports from the state of Baja California Norte that two people had died within 10 days in the custody of federal police in Tijuana. The official death certificate attributed 25-year-old Francisco Díaz Barriga's death to a heart attack. In the case of Enrique Rubio Castañeda, aged 60, the official death certificate gave only "acute withdrawal syndrome" as the cause of death. In both cases, there were well-founded reasons to doubt the causes of death given by the police. Other detainees alleged that the body of Enrique Rubio Castañeda exhibited signs of torture such as inflammation of the genitals, and bruising. Two other young men held at the same detention centre during the same period are also said to have been tortured. Both reportedly had swollen hands, bruising all over their bodies and burns as a result of electric torture with electric prods. Amnesty International knows of no inquiries into these allegations.

MEXICO

In late 1990 Amnesty International received further reports of torture in Baja California Norte state, in the form of detailed testimonies obtained from 86 prisoners in *La Mesa* state penitentiary in Tijuana between July and August 1990. All 86 allege that they confessed to the charges for which they were imprisoned after being tortured by the police. The torture methods described included near-asphyxiation with plastic bags, electric torture, carbonated water forced through the nostrils, beatings and threats. Many of the testimonies are documented with medical certificates noting after-effects which would appear to be consistent with the allegations made. Amnesty International knows of no subsequent investigations into these well-documented claims of torture.

Even when investigations have been conducted into allegations of torture they have rarely resulted in prosecution. In the state of Quintana Roo, for example, federal judicial police agents seem to operate with impunity. Although they have frequently been implicated in human rights abuses, the agents responsible have not been brought to justice. In one case, in which a detainee died, over a year later the investigations have not led to prosecutions: the only police officer arrested, of several implicated, managed to escape and went into hiding. On 6 June 1990 Jorge Argáez, José Pérez and Amílcar Vallejos, three fishermen from Isla Mujeres island in Quintana Roo, were forced into a vehicle at gunpoint by federal anti-narcotics agents and taken to the town of Cancún. While in incommunicado detention they were reportedly interrogated under torture about drugs offences. The following day José Pérez and Amílcar Vallejos were released without charge, although the latter had to be admitted to a local hospital suffering from multiple trauma. That same day, at 6pm, federal judicial police agents dumped Jorge Argáez outside the General Hospital of Cancún. He was admitted to hospital in poor condition and died there two days later. Before dying he gave an account of the torture he said he and his friends had suffered to the doctors treating him.

On 14 June the state congress of Quintana Roo publicly condemned all cases of human rights abuses and called for those responsible for the torture of the fishermen and for the murder of Jorge Argáez to be brought to justice. However, the investigations proceeded slowly. By the end of June only one of the police officers implicated in the incident had been arrested and he managed to escape within a day of his arrest. On 20 June 1990, the Bar Association of Cancún issued a public complaint about flagrant irregularities in the investigations, but as of May 1991 no further progress in the case had been reported.

In another case, in the Federal District, five police agents were charged in connection with the death of a detainee. On 29 March 1989 the Federal District Attorney General's Office admitted that five judicial police agents were responsible for the death in custody of Octavio Hernández Pérez. He had been detained on 26 March and taken to the Public Ministry Agency, in Azcapotzalco, on charges of possessing marijuana. There he was beaten to death during interrogation. His body was later found inside his abandoned car. An autopsy found that he had died from head injuries. Arrest warrants on charges of homicide and related offences were issued on 1 April 1989 for the five officers allegedly

CHAPTER 3

responsible but they had reportedly gone into hiding and, at the time of writing, had not been brought to justice.

In another case, in the state of Durango, the state governor is said to have severely reprimanded the federal judicial police for torturing detainees, but there have been no criminal proceedings against them. The case concerned Luis Angel Tejada Espino, a well-known politician in the state and a member of the ruling Institutional Revolutionary Party, and Gabino Carrillo Monarrez, both of whom were in prison awaiting trial on drugs charges in November 1989. They were apparently removed from the prison, the Centre for Social Rehabilitation, by federal police officers, without the consent of a judge, and taken to the headquarters of the Republic Attorney General's Office in Mexico City. There, they were allegedly tortured by beatings and near-asphyxiation to force them to confess to drugs offences. They were returned to Durango two days later. A formal complaint on their behalf about illegal removal from prison and torture was presented in December 1989, but at time of writing, May 1991, there had been no criminal proceedings against those allegedly responsible for torturing them, nor had their legal situation been reviewed in the light of their allegations that their confessions were made under torture.

One of the few instances in which proceedings have been initiated was a case of death in custody in Aguascalientes state. Ubaldo Santillán Aguilar, aged 22, died on 23 January 1990, the day he was taken into custody in the state capital of Aguascalientes by three state police officers who were investigating a robbery. He was held incommunicado in the local state police headquarters and tortured by being beaten and having his head repeatedly submerged in a water tank. The autopsy report gave the cause of death as "suffocation due to submersion". The state Attorney General promised a full investigation into the case, which he described as an "isolated" incident. However, the director of the state police declared that Ubaldo Santillán Aguilar had died because the police officers under his command had "gone too far". Three police officers were arrested, brought before a judge, and detained on charges of homicide. Two of them had been accused of ill-treatment and causing injuries to detainees in other cases, and one was under investigation as a result. Despite this, both were still in active service at the time of Ubaldo Santillán Aguilar's arrest.

Ineffectiveness of legal remedies

Alleged torture victims can seek redress. But the remedies are seldom effective and they are inaccessible to most people. In addition, as illustrated elsewhere in this report, victims and relatives who do seek redress have been harassed, intimidated and in some cases abducted and tortured.

Defendants or their legal representatives can challenge convictions based on confessions extracted under duress, or otherwise illegally obtained evidence, by making use of the *recurso de amparo* which enables individuals to challenge acts of state or federal authorities which infringe the individual guarantees enshrined in the Constitution. However, this constitutional remedy has been

MEXICO

reported to be ineffective in most claims made by criminal defendants in cases of alleged coercion by law enforcement agents, since the first confession may still be used to convict even when the defendant proves it was forcibly obtained through coercion.

Recurso de amparo is of little use in cases of secret detention because it is only admissible when the authorities responsible for the arrest and the whereabouts of the detainee are known. It is also limited because it only has local jurisdiction. When detainees are moved from one state jurisdiction to another, they or their lawyers must make a further deposition to the new authority.

The remedy of *amparo* is, in any case, inaccessible to the majority of those most in need of protection — many detainees charged with criminal offences and therefore at risk of torture are from the poorest sectors of the population and have neither the resources nor the knowledge to pursue this remedy.

In those cases in which *recurso de amparo* has been granted to a detainee, this has rarely been followed by prosecutions of those responsible for violating their constitutional rights.

Although anyone detained on a criminal charge is guaranteed by law the right to legal counsel during the initial period of detention under the Public Ministry, in practice this right is reserved only for those who are detained in accordance with the law by being presented with an arrest warrant or arrested *flagrante delicto* and immediately brought before a judge and who have the resources to afford legal assistance — a minority of detainees.

It is only after the defendant is presented before a judge that he or she will have a public defence counsel appointed. Provision of such legal counsel is not a state obligation during pre-judicial detention, although defendants do have the right to counsel with a private lawyer or consultant at that stage. In some cases where lawyers have been procured, the lawyers themselves have been obstructed or arrested.

Large sections of the population are not fully aware of their constitutional rights and guarantees and have little means of finding this information themselves. This can only foster the practice of abuses by members of the security forces. That their cases ever reach the public is largely due to the work of independent human rights activists, a development stimulated by the growing concern about human rights in the country.

Juan Ignacio Orozco Villagómez was one of three people detained in the Federal District for questioning in connection with a murder on 28 July 1989. The authorities initially denied that he had been detained despite the fact that his car was seen parked at the Federal District judicial police building. After five days in incommunicado detention, during which period he alleged he was tortured, he was brought before a judge following a *recurso de amparo* petition filed by his relatives. The following day a statement was taken from him without the presence of a defence lawyer — neither he nor his family were apparently informed of the right to have one present. Although the Public Ministry Agent subsequently maintained that a public defence counsel had been present when

CHAPTER 3

Juan Ignacio Orozco Villagómez' statement was taken, over 10 witnesses denied this claim.

The right to seek redress is severely undermined by the fact that victims, witnesses and relatives have been threatened, harassed and sometimes killed, when they attempt to do so. Such efforts to subvert justice are rarely punished. The result of this is that most people who have suffered or witnessed torture or ill-treatment have been too frightened to make official complaints. In addition, human rights activists who document and report on cases of torture and ill-treatment have also been threatened.

In April 1990 Víctor Clark Alfaro, director of the Tijuana Bi-National Human Rights Centre, published the results of an investigation into the torture of children in the custody of the Tijuana juvenile justice system. Seventy-six such cases had been documented between 15 January and 30 March 1990. Forty-seven had allegedly been tortured by the state judicial police, 14 by the municipal police, three by the federal judicial police and 12 by employees of a local juvenile reform centre.

On 13 June 1990 Víctor Clark Alfaro reportedly received an anonymous telephone call threatening him with death because of his investigations. The same day he received a second telephone call warning him to stop his work. He believes that the threats were made by police officers implicated in cases of torture of minors documented in his reports.

In another case, in Mexico City, Mariana Rodríguez Villegas, a secretary, was stopped at gunpoint in the street by a man in civilian clothes and interrogated about the whereabouts of her employer's wife and children. They threatened to kill her employer if he continued his work. Her employer is a well-known journalist and professor, Jorge Castañeda. He had recently published an article implicating the federal police in human rights abuses, to which the government had been forced to respond.

Jorge Castañeda denounced the incident and made an official complaint to the courts. He received a personal telephone call from President Salinas, assuring him that the government was not responsible. Three days later Mariana Rodríguez Villegas, who had initially identified the federal police officers who had threatened her from photographs at the police headquarters, was again stopped in the street and threatened with death if she continued to collaborate with the investigations.

4

Amnesty International's proposals to prevent torture

The United Nations (UN) Convention against Torture and Other Cruel, Inhuman or Degrading Treatment or Punishment, to which Mexico is a State Party, requires the government to take effective legislative, administrative, judicial and other measures at federal and state level to prevent acts of torture and to bring to justice those found responsible of such abuses.

Amnesty International urges the Mexican Government to implement the following recommendations to fulfil its obligations under the Convention. Many of these recommendations call for measures required by international standards for the protection of human rights, including the UN Body of Principles for the Protection of All Persons under Any Form of Detention or Imprisonment. Some of these measures have been formally adopted by the Mexican Government but remain to be fully implemented.

1 Prevent arbitrary arrest

- All arrests should be carried out under strict judicial control and only by authorized personnel.
- Law enforcement officials should adequately identify themselves and present arrest warrants at the time of arrest.
- Everyone should be informed, at the time of arrest, of the specific reasons for their arrest.
- All detainees should also receive an oral and written explanation, in a language they understand, of how to avail themselves of their legal rights, including the right to lodge complaints of ill-treatment.
- The armed forces should be prohibited from arresting, holding in custody or interrogating civilian detainees.
- Failure to adhere to these safeguards should lead to the disciplinary or bringing to justice of those responsible.

2 Prevent incommunicado detention

- All detainees should be brought before a judge promptly after arrest, and within the period stipulated by law.
- Anyone arrested *flagrante delicto* should be immediately brought before a judge.
- All detainees should have access to relatives and lawyers promptly after arrest and regularly throughout their detention or imprisonment.

CHAPTER 4

- The government should provide free legal assistance to defendants without resources. In addition, interpreters should be provided for non-Spanish speaking defendants.
- Relatives should be informed immediately of any arrest and should be kept informed of the detainee's whereabouts at all times.
- Rulings which result from a petition of *recurso de amparo* on cases of detention, including unacknowledged, irregular or arbitrary detention, should be effectively enforceable throughout Mexico.
- Detainees and prisoners should be held only in official, known detention centres, a list of which should be widely publicized.
- Every detention centre should be required to keep a detailed up-to-date record, bound with numbered pages, of the time of arrest and the identities of those who carried out the arrest, as well as the time the detainee appeared before the Public Ministry Agent and before the judicial authority.

3 Provide strict controls over interrogation procedures

- Interrogation should take place in the presence of a defence counsel to ensure that statements taken in evidence from a detainee are given freely and not as a result of coercion.
- In addition to a lawyer, a female officer should be present during interrogation of women detainees.
- Children should only be questioned in the presence of a parent or next of kin.
- The date, time and duration of each period of interrogation should be clearly recorded, as well as the names of all those present during interrogation. These records should be open to judicial scrutiny and to inspection by lawyers and relatives of detainees.
- The government should publish current guidelines of interrogation procedures and periodically review both procedures and practices, inviting submissions and recommendations from civil rights groups, defence lawyers, bar associations and other interested parties.

4 Separate the authorities responsible for detention and interrogation

- There should be a clear and complete separation between the authorities responsible for detention and those responsible for the interrogation of detainees. This would allow an agency not involved in interrogation to supervise the welfare and physical security of detainees.
- The role of the Public Ministry, which is currently responsible for detention, interrogation and prosecution in criminal proceedings, should therefore be revised.

5 Prohibit the use of confessions extracted under torture

- Confessions obtained as a result of torture or other ill-treatment should never be admitted in legal proceedings, except as evidence against the perpetrators.

MEXICO

- Defendants who were convicted on the basis of coerced confessions should have their convictions promptly reviewed.
- In cases where detainees complain that their confessions were extracted under torture, the burden should be on the detaining and interrogating authorities to prove that the confession was voluntary and that torture and ill-treatment did not occur.

6 Implement judicial safeguards

- Judges should be vigorous in examining the legality of detention and the physical condition of defendants, and in investigating all claims of torture.
- International standards pertaining to the judiciary, including those contained in the UN Basic Principles on the Independence of Judiciary, should be incorporated in Mexican law and legal practice in the interests of a genuinely independent and impartial judiciary.

7 Implement judicial supervision of detention

- Any form of detention or imprisonment and all measures affecting the human rights of a detainee or prisoner should be subject to the effective control of a judicial authority.
- The government should take particular care to ensure that detainees who are vulnerable for reasons of age or gender are not tortured, ill-treated or harassed.
- The confinement of children in prisons for adults should be strictly prohibited.
- All detention centres should be visited and inspected regularly by representatives of an independent body. These inspectors should conduct their visits without advance warning.
- Any detainee or prisoner should have the right to communicate freely and in full confidentiality with the inspectors. The inspectors should have unrestricted access to all relevant records and should be authorized to receive and deal with detainees' complaints.
- The inspection body should prepare detailed reports on the findings of each visit, and should ensure that appropriate action is taken to remedy all shortcomings relating to the treatment of detainees and prisoners.
- The inspection body should also make recommendations for improving conditions of detention in accordance with the UN Standard Minimum Rules for the Treatment of Prisoners.

8 Provide adequate medical safeguards

- An independent medical examiner's office should be established, with administrative autonomy, to provide forensic expertise at a national level.
- Medical examinations should be provided to detainees and prisoners on a regular basis and should be performed by independent professionals under the

supervision of a professional association, in accordance with the following principles:
— A medical examination should be carried out on each detainee promptly after arrest and before interrogation.
— Detainees should be medically examined every 24 hours during the period of interrogation; on a frequent and regular basis throughout detention and imprisonment; and immediately before transfer or release.
— These examinations should be performed personally by the authorized doctor, who should explain to the detainee the importance of having a full and contemporary record of his or her condition.
— Detainees should be informed of the importance of these medical examinations in the written notice of their rights.
— Examinations should be carried out in private, exclusively by medical personnel, providing adequate safeguards for the examination of women prisoners.
— Each detainee should have access to a medical officer at any time on the basis of a reasonable request.
— Detailed medical records on detainees should be kept including: weight, state of nutrition, visible marks on the body, psychological state and complaints about health or treatment received.
— These records should be confidential but should be communicated, at the request of the detainee, to a legal advisor, his or her family, or the authorities charged with investigating the treatment of prisoners.
— Each detainee should be entitled to private examinations by his or her own doctor at the request of the detainee or the detainee's lawyer or family.
• The medical examination of alleged victims of human rights abuses should only be conducted in the presence of independent witnesses: a health professional designated by the family, the legal representative of the victim or a professional designated by an independent medical association.
• Forensic doctors should be provided with the training and resources necessary for the diagnosis of all forms of torture and ill-treatment.
• In all cases of deaths in custody, forensic investigations should conform to international standards including the UN Principles on the Effective Prevention and Investigation of Extra-Legal, Arbitrary and Summary Executions.

9 Investigate all reports of torture

• All reports of suspected torture or ill-treatment should be promptly, thoroughly and impartially investigated.
• The investigating authority should have: the power to obtain all information necessary to the inquiry; adequate financial and technical resources for effective investigation; and the authority to oblige those accused of torture to appear and testify.
• Any government official who suspects that torture has been committed

should report it to the relevant authorities, which should fully investigate all such reports.
- The absence of a complaint by the victim or relatives should not deter investigation.
- The National Human Rights Commission should be given formal and full independence and should be able to demonstrate that it is free from governmental pressure and influence.
- The commission should be provided with adequate resources and sufficient investigative powers to carry out its task effectively.
- The commission's recommendations should be implemented by the authorities responsible for instigating criminal prosecutions, who should be held accountable if they fail to do so.
- The involvement or complicity of health professionals in the torture and ill-treatment of detainees should be thoroughly and impartially investigated. Disciplinary proceedings should be instituted against medical personnel found to have breached the UN Principles of Medical Ethics. Any criminal act found to have been committed should be referred to the courts.

10 Bring torturers to justice

- Any law enforcement agent or person acting under the direction of law enforcement agents who is responsible for committing torture, or for ordering, encouraging or condoning the practice of torture, should be brought to justice.
- Any law enforcement agent charged in connection with the crime of torture should be immediately suspended from duties directly related to arresting, guarding or interrogating detainees. If convicted, they should be automatically dismissed from duty, in addition to whatever other punishment is imposed by the court.
- The crime of torture should not be subject to any statute of limitations.

11 Protect victims and witnesses

- The government should ensure that all necessary measures are taken to prevent attacks on or threats against victims of torture and their relatives, witnesses to human rights violations and human rights monitors in Mexico; and that all those responsible for such actions be brought to justice.

12 Compensate the victims of torture

- All victims of torture should receive medical treatment and rehabilitation where necessary, and financial compensation commensurate with the abuse inflicted.
- In cases where a detainee's death is shown to be the result of torture or ill-treatment the deceased's relatives should receive compensatory and exemplary damages.

CHAPTER 4

13 Promote respect for human rights

• An absolute prohibition of torture and ill-treatment as crimes under domestic law should be visibly displayed in every detention centre in the country.

• The government should adopt and publish a code of conduct for all law enforcement agents who exercise powers of detention and arrest. This code should conform to the UN Code of Conduct for Law Enforcement Officials and the UN Basic Principles on the Use of Force and Firearms by Law Enforcement Officials.

• In addition to categorically prohibiting the use of torture and ill-treatment, the code should ensure that law enforcement agents oppose the use of torture or ill-treatment, if necessary by refusing to carry out orders to inflict such treatment on detainees, and report any such abuses of authority to their superior officers and, where necessary, to the authorities vested with review or remedial powers.

• Breaches of the code should result in specified disciplinary sanctions and criminal prosecution of the agents involved.

• The government should ensure that all law enforcement agents and members of the armed forces receive adequate training on human rights standards, both domestic and international, and the means for their protection.

14 Promote human rights awareness

• Human rights education should be included in the curriculum at every stage of the education system.

• There should be a broad program aimed at promoting human rights awareness among all sectors of society, particularly among those sectors most vulnerable to abuses of authority including the non-Spanish speaking ethnic minorities.

15 Abide by international law

• Domestic law and practice should fully conform with international human rights instruments including human rights conventions ratified by Mexico, as well as the UN Body of Principles for the Protection of All Persons under Any Form of Detention or Imprisonment and the UN Principles on the Effective Prevention and Investigation of Extra-Legal, Arbitrary and Summary Executions.

16 Recognize international procedures for the protection of human rights

• The government should ratify the (First) Optional Protocol of the International Covenant on Civil and Political Rights, which allows individuals who have exhausted all domestic legal remedies to submit a written complaint to the UN Human Rights Committee alleging that their rights under the Covenant have been violated.

• The government should declare, under Article 22 of the UN Convention against Torture and Other Cruel, Inhuman or Degrading Treatment or Punishment,

MEXICO

that it recognizes the full competence of the UN Committee against Torture to investigate complaints of human rights violations lodged by individuals who have exhausted all domestic legal remedies.

• The government should recognize the jurisdiction of the Inter-American Court of Human Rights over all matters relating to the interpretation or application of human rights safeguards contained in the American Convention.

POST-SCRIPT:

Shortly after going to press, Amnesty International received news of major developments in two of the most prominent cases documented in the report, which are detailed below.

Lawyer Francisco Antonio Valencia Fontes, Enrique Machi Ramírez and Armando Machi Bustamante were released on 15 June after spending 18 months in prison (see page 33). They were released after the Republic Attorney General's Office dropped the charges against them on the recommendation of the National Human Rights Commission. Two others arrested in connection with the case, José Luis Antillón and Juan Alfonso Ortiz Gōmez, were also released. Amnesty International remains concerned that those responsible for their torture have not been suspended from their duties pending investigation, that they have not been brought to justice and that the victims and their relatives have received no compensation for the abuses suffered.

Magdaleno Vera Garcia and Carlos Valencia Morfín were released without charge on 26 June, after over 13 months' detention. Both alleged they have been tortured by federal judicial police agents to confess to drug charges. Their release, together with that of Salomón Mendoza Barajas and Javier Rosiles Martínez, had been recommended by the National Human Rights Commission in November 1990 (see page 12). Amnesty International has noted that a federal judicial police agent accused of participating in torturing them—and who was later accused of involvement in the death under torture of Pedro Yescas Martínez (see page 20)—was arrested in June 1991. It is continuing to monitor the investigations into the allegations of torture, to urge that all those responsible be brought to justice and that proper compensation be provided to the victims and their relatives.